Take Me with You

"Scott Jackson knows that good storytelling helps people discover their passions and connect with great causes. In *Take Me with You*, he tells his own story, explaining how a child's decision to run away from an abusive father in the middle of a Kansas snowstorm changed his life and made him a fighter for justice and equity. Scott understands the power of the personal narrative, and he uses it to weave a compelling call to action to address the toughest development challenges of the 21st century."

—Dr. Christopher Elias
President of the Global Development Division
Bill & Melinda Gates Foundation, former President
and CEO of PATH

"I first read an early draft of *Take Me with You* at least a half dozen years ago. It was spellbinding then. But it has matured since then, and now is the time for the story to come forth. Today, more than ever, we need this personal account of how courage, persistence, and love overcame abuse and racism, and how these qualities are central to the unprecedented flourishing of global philanthropy. We are indeed building a better, safer world and Scott Jackson's life story is no small part of that effort."

—Dr. Jack Faris
formerly Director of Community Strategies,
Bill & Melinda Gates Foundation

"From the moment I met Scott Jackson in the fall of 1976 my life has been enriched and inspired by his contagious energy and passion. Now *Take Me with You* inspires its readers. Scott Jackson's book is an important combination of call for action and a wonderful read that tells a meaningful story."

—John Oppenheimer
CEO of Columbia Hospitality

"When Scott Jackson worked with me at World Vision, I saw his heart for vulnerable children before I knew his story—and what a remarkable story it is! A young white boy caught in the midst of racial discrimination and abuse in America's Midwest in the 1960s makes a daring cross-country escape to find a new life in an African-American community in the Pacific Northwest. Yet the things that could have broken him instead made him stronger in his faith, his compassion, and his desire to be a catalyst for justice. This book is a riveting and amazing read."

—RICHARD STEARNS
President of World Vision U.S.
and author of *The Hole in Our Gospel*

"*Take Me with You* spoke to my heart. Scott Jackson writes of growing up as a young White boy in the Midwest during the early 60s when communities across the United States were confronting the harsh realities of racial inequality. Scott lived just this side of the railroad tracks with an abusive father who crushed the very spirit of those he loved best: Scott and his mother. In their attempt to escape the terror of an abusive home, Scott and his mother sought physical and spiritual sanctuary within the Black community living on the other side of the tracks, and discovered pathways to healing that speak to humanity's great capacity for acceptance and compassion and, yes, love.

In a deceptively simple style, Scott recounts his journey with grace and humility. Through his story we come to appreciate that Scott, by virtue of his deep faith and unique life experiences, has been able to find 'the charity within.' How extraordinary to have woven his story as a survivor of abuse and as a kid growing up in a biracial family with insights gathered across the years working as a leader in global development and as an expert on US philanthropy! We should all thank Scott for writing *Take Me with You*. Such an authentic voice is rare, and the promise of his story is one that we need to realize today. I thank him for including the International Center for Research on Women as a noteworthy charity in the book. We are honored."

—SARAH DEGNAN KAMBOU
President of the International Center
for Research on Women

"Scott Jackson's *Take Me with You* is an amazing tale that is truly made captivating by his early struggles with racism and how that shaped his commitment and career to serving others. As a child, he faced difficult choices involving his biological father and mother's marriage to a black preacher that complicated his life but eventually proved inspirational. Often it's not the smooth sailing through life, but a tough and bruising journey that builds character and leads to higher achievements. Scott Jackson's story is revealing of his spirit and determination to make a difference in people's lives, clearly demonstrated throughout the book and by his senior executive positions with the world's most prominent organizations. *Take Me with You* will bring value and inspiration to anyone who reads it."

—DON BONKER
Executive Director APCO Worldwide
Former U.S. Congressman

Take Me with You

Take Me with You

One Person's Journey to Find the Charity Within

Scott Jackson

SelectBooks, Inc.
New York

This edition published by SelectBooks, Inc.
For information address SelectBooks, Inc., New York, New York.

First Edition

ISBN 978-1-59079-392-3

Library of Congress Cataloging-in-Publication Data

Names: Jackson, Scott, (Philanthropist), author.
Title: Take me with you / Scott Jackson.
Description: New York : SelectBooks, 2017.
Identifiers: LCCN 2016029245 | ISBN 9781590793923 (hardback)
Subjects: LCSH: Jackson, Scott, (Philanthropist) | Philanthropists--United
  States--Biography. | Fund raising--United States. | Leadership. | BISAC:
  BIOGRAPHY & AUTOBIOGRAPHY / Personal Memoirs.
Classification: LCC HV28.J33 J33 2017 | DDC 361.7/4092 [B] --dc23 LC record
available at https://lccn.loc.gov/2016029245

Book design by Janice Benight

Manufactured in the United States of America
10 9 8 7 6 5 4 3 2 1

This is my story, my song, dedicated to the Reverend Jefferson Jackson—
Beloved Pastor, Husband, and Father.

To Sydney, the love of Jefferson's life and my mom,
who never wavered in her commitment to "Take Me with You."

To all of us who persevere to find the "charity within,"
regardless of life's circumstances.

Contents

Introduction

I wanted to share my story because it has influenced my own commitment to help others realize their full potential and contribute to a better, safer world. My goal is to offer a message of hope and encourage you to embark on your own journey to serve others and spark positive change—in whatever way you can—because every life matters and there are so many in need around the globe.

As I write this, I have the privilege of serving as President and CEO of Global Impact. Global Impact's mission as a global nonprofit organization is to "build partnerships and resources for the world's most vulnerable people." Our amazing staff is comprised predominately of talented Gen Xers and millennials. Together, with our board of directors and our partners, we are all about "growing global philanthropy" and supporting those organizations—public, private, and nonprofit—that tackle the world's most pressing problems.

Over the past 60 years, Global Impact has raised more than $1.8 billion, supports annually 450 public and private sector partners and their respective employee giving campaigns, receives funds from hundreds of thousands of donors, and has distributed contributions to thousands of charities here in the United States and around the world. The Global Impact charity alliance supports the work of more than 120 international nongovernmental organizations (INGOs), including Doctors without Borders, UNICEF, Care, Heifer International, Save the Children, and World Vision. The resources we raise have contributed to meeting the needs of approximately 400 million people in 200-plus countries.

Before joining Global Impact, my own career journey has included holding leadership positions in global development in the public, private, and nonprofit sectors. The range of issues I have worked on include at-risk youth in America's largest cities and underserved rural communities; responding to 9/11, Katrina, and the HIV AIDS pandemic; funding for new vaccine development, including for meningitis in Africa and malaria worldwide; raising funds and awareness for combating HIV AIDS; and the Syrian refugee crisis. I have worked on presidential campaigns, and I was a founding member as a nonprofit leader for the ONE Campaign to make poverty history. I have traveled and worked in more than 65 countries, opening up new markets, promoting international trade, responding to crises, and supporting long-term development. But before I chose this path of philanthropy, I lived a life of struggle and hardship and had to overcome adversity, which is why I feel so personally connected to this work.

Bono launching the ONE Campaign in 2004 in Philadelphia with Dikembe Mutombo in the background

Scott with President Clinton. *President Clinton presenting me with a Clinton Global Initiative Commitment to Action in 2005.*

My Personal Story

My family lived outside Kansas City, and for much of our time together my dad preached at Edwardsville Christian Church. We lived in the parsonage, a two-bedroom box just south of the railroad tracks that separated the white and black parts of town. I grew up during the American Civil Rights Movement, a time when my family fell apart and my future became uncertain—a struggle between parents and different ways of life. As the civil rights movement heated up, my mom crossed the tracks whenever she could. For that and for other indiscernible reasons, Dad abused her. My background was the same as thousands—even millions—of other at-risk youth like me who had to overcome barriers of race, religion, and broken families.

During the winter of my thirteenth year, I ran away from home on a cold night in early February and disappeared into a Kansas snowstorm. By running away, I found a new life, and this journey also marked a rebirth for my mom and for Jefferson Jackson, the black Baptist minister with a tenth-grade education who fell in love with my mother. He became a father figure to me and raised me. In our lives together we were often in hiding and almost always impoverished. From this beginning it seemed unlikely I would achieve the kind of worldly success that most privileged people expect. But we had love and a dedication to each other that is the foundation of well-being.

Because of the influence of my parents and others as I grew up, I chose to support the causes for justice and well-being for people throughout the world. My story tells how my own difficult childhood brought me to the world of global development, where I was given the opportunities to change the world and work with many others in doing so. I was able to rise to the highest levels of leadership in the international nongovernmental organizational sector, serving as Senior Vice President of World Vision US and as the Vice President of PATH Worldwide, before joining Global Impact. My work has often been behind the scenes, with a focus on building partnerships, raising funds, advocacy, and visibility for those on the front lines.

My childhood escape from abuse has influenced my present work and driven my personal commitment to leave a lasting mark on humanity. My story is about one boy who chooses love, forgiveness, and "finding the charity within." This meant letting go of the anger and regret about what could have been and choosing the positive to be a force for good. This is the same choice we each must make if we are to respect all people regardless of gender, race, socio-economic position, family origin, where a person is born, or the circumstances in which they find themselves. Each of us can harness the power of our own personal struggles to influence others and to have our own impact on the world.

Scott Jackson is my chosen name, not the one I was born with. I took the name of my stepfather, the Reverend Jefferson Jackson, for reasons that will become clear as my story unfolds. Many of the events I recount took place more than forty years ago but have shaped the man I have become. I'm the sum of my story, this memoir rooted in love, faith, and moral courage.

The Global Goals for Sustainable Development

The year 2016 began with two historic global agreements that shaped sustainable development as never before. The first of these agreements is the 2030 Agenda for Sustainable Development adopted by the United Nations General Assembly in September, 2015. The 17 Global Goals for Sustainable Development and their 169 targets were embraced by an unprecedented 193 countries, and, in the words of the United Nations Development Program UNDP, their mission is "to end poverty, hunger, and inequality, take action on climate change and the environment, improve access to health and education, build strong institutions and partnerships, and more."

The Global Goals are the result of consultations in more than 130 countries with civil society, the public and private sector, and they replace the Millennium Development Goals (MDGs) that came before them. I believe it's important to know exactly what the global goals are, and where help is most urgently needed, if you are hoping to make a real difference in the world.

Understanding each of the Global Goals can help you focus on those areas that are meaningful to you if you wish to connect on a personal level to those charities or organizations that are addressing global needs throughout the world. The 17 Global Goals include:

- no poverty
- zero hunger
- good health and well-being
- quality education
- gender equality
- clean water and sanitation
- affordable and clean energy
- decent work and economic growth
- industry, innovation and infrastructure
- reduced inequalities
- sustainable cities and communities
- responsible consumption and production
- climate action
- life below water
- life on land
- peace and justice; strong institutions
- partnerships for the goals

More broadly, the Global Goals are intended to bring an end to poverty, inequality, and injustice and to reverse climate change.

The second of the two international agreements is the "Paris Agreement" on climate change, a treaty negotiated and adopted by representatives of 195 countries at the 2015 United Nations Climate Change Conference (COP 21) held in Paris in December 2015. The White House declared it "the most ambitious climate change agreement in history." The Paris Agreement recognizes two fundamental principles in its preamble: (1) "that climate change represents an urgent and potentially irreversible threat to human societies and the planet and thus requires the widest possible cooperation by all countries"; and (2) "that deep reductions in global emissions will be required in order to achieve the ultimate objective of the Convention and emphasizing the need for urgency in addressing climate change."

As the White House noted about the Paris Agreement, which went into effect on November 4, 2016, "The deal builds on the unprecedented participation of 187 countries that submitted post-2020 climate action targets in advance of the meeting. . . . The Agreement moves beyond dividing the world into outdated categories of developed and developing countries and instead directs all parties to prepare, communicate, and maintain successive and ambitious nationally determined climate targets."

Neither of these global development agreements will change the world for the better on their own. In fact, it is clear that the funding commitments and programs necessary to achieve these goals cannot be carried out by governments or large institutional donors alone. The public and private sectors both must play a role. Philanthropic contributions must be leveraged by private investments and business solutions. Every person on the planet has a role to play. The goals are not just for less developed countries but for every country and population, rich and poor. The gap between the rich and poor has never been greater. We must make these goals personal if we are to have true equity.

The Sustainable Development Goals are designed to fulfill a vision. According to the United Nations, that vision is as follows:

> *In these Goals and targets, we are setting out a supremely ambitious and transformational vision. We envisage a world free of poverty, hunger, disease and want, where all life can thrive. We envisage a world free of fear and violence. A world with universal literacy. A world with equitable and universal access to quality education at all levels, to health care and social protection. A world where physical, mental and social well-being are assured. A world where we reaffirm our commitments regarding the human right to safe drinking water and sanitation and where there is improved hygiene; and where food is sufficient, safe, affordable and nutritious. A world where human habitats are safe, resilient and sustainable and where there is universal access to affordable, reliable, and sustainable energy.*

This vision needs you in order to succeed.

About This Book

Take Me with You is a call to action to help those in need, especially children. I hope that my story will inspire you to do whatever you can to change a life for the better, by making a personal connection to a larger global issue. After each chapter of my personal narrative, I have included short essays, or what I think of as "global connections," for the reader that highlight the most pressing challenges of our time, some of which I have encountered personally, as well as the positive measures being taken to combat these challenges. I will highlight the particular Global Goal out of the 17 that correlates to the problem outlined in the essay to make the connection to this global problem by giving you a better sense of how the Goals were specifically developed to tackle concrete issues like hunger, gender equality, or access to clean water.

You will then find information about some of the charitable organizations working on the front lines for each of the Global Goals—whether it's to eliminate poverty, bring health care to those in need, aid refugees in war-torn countries, or empower and educate women—in case you want to get involved personally in a cause that is meaningful to you.

Every child—whether in the United States or in less developed countries—deserves to have a fighting chance in life. You have the choice to live your life in a way that will change another person's life for the better . . . and maybe transform your own along the way.

Take Me with You

CHAPTER ONE

When I Was Little

Edwardsville, Kansas, brushes the western border of Kansas City. It's a sliver of a town hammered between busy railroad tracks and the Kansas River. I moved to Edwardsville with my parents when I was eight months old, shortly after Dad finished seminary and he took his first preaching job. The three of us lived in the church parsonage. The house stood half a block from the railroad tracks. When the trains came, and they came often, family photos rattled on the walls and the entire house shook. Some of the trains pulled two hundred cars and seemed to last forever. To this day, I remember how loud they were. Years later, I wondered if that's why so many secrets stayed in our household for so long—people just couldn't hear them.

The parsonage squeezed two bedrooms, a bathroom, living room, kitchen, and laundry room into six hundred square feet, if that. On most days, Dad walked the four blocks to church across the tracks and highway. Along the way, he passed the town's old city hall, a stone building erected just a few paces off the rail line in 1917. After work, Dad stopped at the post office and store, the town's two main attractions. What Edwardsville lacked in population and culture, it made up for in small-town convenience. In 1958, the year we moved to town, Edwardsville was eight square blocks and home to five hundred people. During the entire time we lived there, I don't think we ever locked our doors.

The parsonage where we lived in Edwardsville, Kansas

I got to know Edwardsville better than anyone. By the time I turned six, I had ridden my bike through every gravel alley in town too many times to count. My bike was one of the best gifts ever. Normally, I received my presents on Christmas Eve. I was an only child and I would always tell my mom I couldn't wait. She couldn't either. I had been hoping for a bicycle, and not just any bike. I wanted a two-wheeler banana seat, high-handle bars special. I had been off training wheels for a couple of years and was ready for a real bike. That Christmas Eve there were other presents nestled under the tree but no bicycle.

The next morning Mom woke me and said, "Hurry, Santa left one more present!"

We made our way out of the house, across the small snow-covered yard, and into the garage. There it rested: the bike of my dreams. We opened the garage door and my dachshund Dewey and I took off. I thought of stopping by Jackie Shumaker's house or several other homes in the neighborhood, but I didn't have close friends. Not everyone wanted to spend time with the pastor's kid who wasn't that cool. But I didn't care—I had my new bike, my best friend, Dewey, and the cold air on my cheeks. I was so fast on that bike that Dewey had a hard time keeping up with his short, little legs.

The air was brisk and the gravel alleyways were frozen. Edwardsville was a small town, and I knew every street. When I got tired of riding, I hung out by the tracks. Sometimes I'd collect rusty rail spikes or pick wildflowers growing in the dirt. Other times, I'd sneak through a thicket of trees along the bank of the Kansas River and watch the water pass. In that part of the state, the river runs wide and slow on its way to Kansas City. As long as I stayed in Edwardsville, I felt safe, and I felt safest on my bike in the alleyways away from the little parsonage called home.

My other favorite place when I was little, the one I might not tell anyone about, was my mother's lap, which I crawled into whenever I could. The rocking chair was our favorite resting place. I can still remember the squeak, lift, and pull of the family rocker, a gift from Grandpa Hughes, and the floor lamp turned on next to the rocker in the evenings when we would read together. My mom smelled like the wildflowers in the Kansas countryside. She opened the worn cover of the dark blue book and read the stories and showed me pictures from the Bible.

My mom was beautiful. She had long brown hair, a slender neck, and extraordinary green eyes. One recurring dream I had as a child was seeing my mom on a street corner in a blue dress with a string of pearls around her neck. Her hair was naturally a dark brunette and styled like a movie star. She was in many ways an "Elizabeth Taylor" figure, always trying to do the right or proper thing but really only interested in being loved for who she was.

Mom liked living in Edwardsville because it was close to her parents. Grandma and Grandpa Hughes lived on the other side of

Baby Scott sitting on his mother's lap

Sydney Lou looking like a movie star of the 60s and changing her hair with the times

Kansas City, across the Missouri state line. During my childhood, I spent every day with Mom. We'd hop in her white Volkswagen VW and drive to the end of some rural road or down a quiet highway. Sometimes we'd stop and stare across fields grown dense with sunflowers. If we stayed long enough, we could see the flowers' huge yellow heads turn with the sun. Mom liked getting away, but she almost always had a destination. More often than parking along the sunflower fields, we parked next to homes even smaller than our own. Inevitably, children would be running in the yard or sitting alone in the distance.

As a pastor's wife, Mom made it her job to help our poorest neighbors. In the great expanse of rolling hills and farm country I once called home, that meant Negroes. Just writing that word haunts my memory. I only use it now because in the place I grew up, in the time I grew up, that's what almost everyone called black people, if not something worse.

That's how it was in Enid, Oklahoma, too, where Mom and Dad first met at Phillips University during auditions for *Family Portrait*, the opening play of Mom's freshman year. Phillips was the top college for members of the Disciples of Christ Church. Built in an old alfalfa field, the campus stood as a temple of higher education in a community otherwise ruled by farmhands. Huge dust clouds blow through Enid, Oklahoma, and when a dust storm hit, students covered their mouths with shirt collars or handkerchiefs and raced inside to avoid suffocating in clouds of wind-whipped dirt.

My mother, Sydney Lou Hughes, was the apple of her daddy's eye. Most folks called her father "Whitey," or if you didn't know him too well, Gilbert. Whitey was the consummate entrepreneur and salesman. He had three sisters and a brother named "Red," and Whitey helped to raise them all. Whitey, a towhead, and Red, a redhead, were inseparable. They were in business together until Red died from alcoholism. Whitey almost always wore a dark suit and tie, which set off his hair. It was so blonde it appeared white in the sun.

Whitey had more small businesses than anyone could count. He and my grandmother went bankrupt once during the Great Depression years, only to get back up on their feet and start again. Whitey was well connected to the business and political interests in Missouri.

Thanks to my grandmother, Pauline, Whitey became a God-fearing, church-going community leader. She had been a teacher from Branson, Missouri, and was known as "Dick" the tomboy. My Grandpa Gilbert fell in love with her and they married. One early morning soon after they were married, Whitey's friends and brother Red brought him home drunk. Pauline promptly told Whitey that if he ever got up that way again, he needn't come home. He never did, and he joined her in church on Sundays.

Whitey and Pauline had two natural children, Sydney Lou and Irwin. Years later, they adopted two more children, Patty and Ricky, who had been abandoned, and they helped to raise and put through school many more children along the way. Irwin was a sickly child and school came hard for him. Grandma nursed him to health and helped him with school, which left Sydney Lou often on her own. She was vivacious, gregarious, intelligent, creative, and just as quick as Irwin wasn't. She talked at six months and skipped kindergarten and first grade, starting school in the second grade.

Whitey's great joy in life was his daughter, Sydney Lou, my mom, and he did everything he could to spoil her and make sure that she knew she could do anything she took a mind to in the world. It took every ounce of discipline Pauline could muster to keep Sydney from marrying a local boy and make sure she was sent off to a good Christian college, Phillips University. So off she went, leaving her high school sweetheart behind.

Grandpa Whitey and Grandma Pauline   *Grandma Pauline's favorite photo*

It wasn't long before my mom fell for her future husband. She found Dad funny and good-looking. Back in college, he still had a medium build with large shoulders, a round face, and dark brown eyes that matched his black hair. He was popular and named the friendliest in his class.

Dad was elected sophomore vice president; he became a member of his class leadership council. A picture from an old yearbook shows him on a bench in the sun with his fellow class officers. He's wearing a white dress shirt, a tie, and glasses, and he's smiling so his upper teeth show. To Sydney Lou Hughes, he seemed perfect.

Although she barely cracked a book, Sydney Lou made good grades and was cast in every drama production on campus. The Elizabeth Taylor look-alike could act, too.

Excitement and promise filled the courtship. Mom fell in love with a man who she hoped would make her laugh and feel safe. Soon Sydney and Dad were holding hands and smiling as they walked the neat cement paths and hallways of the gray stone buildings at Phillips.

Dad's parents lived in Ponca City, Oklahoma, about twenty-five miles south of the Kansas border. His father was a military veteran and was the manager of a paint store. His mom was a stay-at-home mom and school secretary. They owned a small home and attended a local Disciples of Christ First Christian Church. In high school, Dad wrestled and played football. During hot summer days on the practice field, temperatures soared into the hundreds.

When Sydney Lou met Dad's parents for the first time during a visit to Ponca City, the four of them attended church together. Much like the congregation Mom had grown up in, the members of Dad's home church were all white. Shortly after that first visit, Dad proposed.

But he had to go to Claycomo, Missouri, to meet Mom's parents first. She grew up in the northeastern outskirts of Kansas City where Whitey and Pauline, by then, owned a used furniture store. The store sat opposite the family home on a seven-acre farm. Across the highway, a Ford assembly plant drove the Claycomo economy. Grandma and Grandpa owned the farm, the store, and the house. In the wake of World War II, other homes popped up nearby, but Grandma and Grandpa's place became a local landmark.

Grandpa Hughes built a barn behind the house, where Grandma raised horses and chickens. After the Great Depression, Grandpa refused to deposit money in a bank. He stashed cash around the farm instead. When he could, he traded furniture for goods and favors. His favorite currency was all about making a deal, even better when he helped out the other person.

Grandma Hughes was a steadfast believer. During her free time, she often sat at the family's dining room table, a thick slab of maple, and wrote sermons she gave to a local pastor. More than anything, Grandma wanted her daughter to marry a preacher, and she was thrilled when Sydney brought Dad home from college. When he asked for their daughter's hand in marriage, Whitey and Pauline gladly said yes.

To hear Mom tell it, the wedding was perfect. The ceremony took place at Liberty Christian Church, an old landmark built of red

brick and limestone. A trio of stained-glass windows filled the sanctuary and showered more than two hundred attendees in multicolored light. Mom carried a bouquet of white roses down the aisle in a
white dress with a short train. She and Dad knew fewer than half the
guests. Though the wedding celebrated his daughter and new son-
in-law, it gave Grandpa a chance to strengthen his business. If you
knew Whitey Hughes back then, you probably made the guest list.

A few days after their wedding, Mom and Dad drove to Wich-
ita and spent the summer working as youth counselors. When they
returned to school, they moved into married-student housing. In 1957
Dad finished seminary and Mom completed her first year teaching
high school. They also learned that Mom was pregnant.

I was born in Saint Mary's Hospital on October 11, 1957, less than
two miles from Phillips University. Dad brought Mom flowers, and
the two of them talked about how having a baby changed everything. The following June, we moved to the parsonage in Edwardsville. During this time, Mom kept a journal about our lives together
and about my growing up. Reading through it years later, I got the
sense that she and Dad were happy. Mom wrote about how I slept in
a century-old cradle passed through the family, about trips we took to
a nearby park, and about how I first said "Daddy" when I was nine
months old. Our lives revolved around the church calendar, and Dad
quickly became one of Edwardsville's most respected citizens.

Not long after my second birthday, my life nearly ended when I
was very ill. When Mom measured my temperature at 104 degrees,
she filled the bathtub with ice water and lifted me inside. When the
fever persisted, she called a doctor to the house. He prescribed peni-
cillin and told my parents to get me to the hospital immediately. Further tests confirmed the doctor's diagnosis of spinal meningitis. The
recommended cure was antibiotics for the short term and sunshine
for a full recovery.

That spring, Mom and Grandma Hughes flew with me to Arizona.
It was March, and snow covered the ground as we left Kansas. I

remember my mom and Grandma Pauline putting me on a plane with them to Tucson, Arizona, for healthy sunshine. My mom and grandmom got sick on the bumpy ride, so without them noticing, I left my seat, slipped away, and went down the aisle to the front of the plane to make an announcement.

"Ladies and gentleman, I want everyone to meet my mom and grandma," I said, as they were cowering over a sick bag in their seats.

The streets of Tucson were just what the doctor ordered. I escaped again with my six shooters on both sides when I joined a staged bank robbery already in progress. I was promptly shot by the sheriff and dutifully fell over in the dust and was taken to jail. Afterward, the sheriff brought me an ice cream cone as a reward for such a fine performance before I was returned to my mother for safekeeping.

We stayed near Tucson for eighteen days. Mom wrote to Dad often. Years later, I found one of those letters inside her old journal. It was written in blue pen and filled two sheets of what appeared to be motel stationary. Mom's handwriting, small and neat, had faded only slightly through the years:

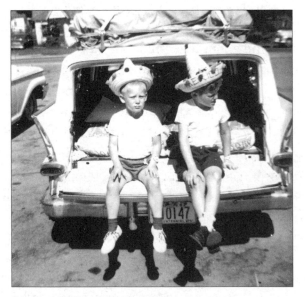

Scott and Ricky camping in Mexico

Dearest One,

We spent the entire day in the sun, and Scottie has a nice sunburn on his face and a slight pink on his arms. We still have the rented car so we drove out to "Old Tucson." They staged a robbery and capture by the Marshall when we first got there & Scottie went wild. He is like a bird just out of a cage. He has run until he could run no more . . . and eaten like a horse. I love you very very much & miss you terribly, but I'm convinced Scottie will be a big healthy new boy with a little of this medicine.

How is snow? I hope it's gone so our meeting will be a wonderful success. I will be praying for its success. I love you so very much.

Good night, sweetheart.
All my love,
Sydney

I recovered completely from my illness. In July that year, our family drove to Texas and Mexico for a two-week vacation. We camped along the way. Mom's journal recalls boat rides, deep-sea fishing, and water skiing. Grandma and Grandpa Hughes joined us with Ricky and Patty, who were both a little older than me, and we became quick friends. A small black-and-white photo taken during that trip shows Ricky and me sitting on the tailgate of the Nash station wagon. Luggage and a giant tarp cover the roof of the car. We're both wearing white T-shirts, shorts, and big straw hats with "Mexico" written on the brims.

Later that year, Mom took me on a much shorter trip. Outside the Kansas City airport, she held me in her arms as Richard Nixon and his wife, Pat, arrived for a presidential campaign stop. As they walked past, Pat Nixon plucked a rose from a huge bouquet and handed it to me. That November, Richard Nixon lost to John F. Kennedy.

I remember another day from around this time, when Mom and I spent hours preparing a roast for dinner. I remember feeling excited about Dad coming home. The smell of meat, vegetables, and potatoes

filled the parsonage. Shortly after Dad arrived, he began yelling when
he noticed the cans of food in the kitchen cabinet were out of order.

"You can't even keep the cabinets neat," he said nastily.

"Well, I've made you dinner," Mom replied.

"Yeah, well, you can't even keep this kitchen clean. We need to
clean up this mess."

"You can clean it up, but we're going to eat."

Dad threw one of the cans down and screamed, "I'm not going
to eat until I get this cleaned up!"

Mom proceeded to empty the entire cabinet onto the floor. "Go
to hell!" she yelled. She threw the silverware drawer at him and tried
to run past.

Dad pushed Mom across the room and began to shake her. As
Mom fought back, screams filled the house. I began to cry uncontrollably. Dad's strength and weight overpowered Mom easily. Chaos
filled the house. I had been setting our tiny card table with silverware.

I said, "Stop it. Stop it!" I covered my ears with my hands to try
to drown out the noise. I still had a fork in my left hand. The next
thing I knew, I was banging the large carving fork against an upright
piano in the living room. Ivory shards flew from the piano keys with
each clang of the fork. Suddenly, Mom ran through the living room.
Dad chased her. His rage bulged from his neck and temples in thick
veins of hate. Mom slammed shut the bathroom door. Dad pounded
on it with both fists.

When Dad finally returned to the kitchen, he looked at me and
said, "Don't worry yourself about it. Your mom just got upset with
me, and now I have to clean it up. Go to your room." He knelt down
and began to pick up the cans and silverware.

We never did eat the dinner Mom had so lovingly prepared. For
the rest of our lives together, the broken piano keys reminded me of
that night and when the façade of our happy home life abruptly ended.

Dad began to hit Mom regularly. I often woke to the sounds of
his abuse. Closed in my room, I trembled in fear. In that tiny house,

everything seemed so close, as if Dad were reaching through the darkness and hitting me, too.

———————————

I remember only two nursery rhymes: "The little boy who lived down the drain," not lane, and "inkin, blinkin, and nod," as I called it. I didn't have much of a childhood, and I had to grow up fast. But my mom would sing those songs to me when I was upset. The happy times from my boyhood consisted of my mother and me and the parallel lives we lived—imaginary and real. The sad times involved my mother and father, which invariably resulted in something awful and inexplicable.

I created imaginary friends. I was an only child with a vivid imagination, and they gave me a way to escape into a different world. I would never eat peas because they were my friends. I did my best to keep them safe from the flood waters caused when the gravy broke through the dam held up by mashed potatoes. There was also Mrs. Wrighley, my grown-up imaginary friend. We always set a place for her at the table and would never leave in the car until she had joined us.

One day, my mom stopped after going a short distance down the road and said, "Oh, we forgot Mrs. Wrighley!"

I responded, "It's okay, Mom. I shot her and she is now dead."

Imagination was critical to my survival. I could imagine a happy home, friends, and loved ones. The most important way Mom and I endured our situation was that she kept our lives focused on others and the world around us in a way that crowded out an unhappy and violent home. We could be happy outside.

In 1963, instead of starting kindergarten like most kids my age, I began first grade. That same fall, Mom started teaching at Bonner Springs High School, four miles west of Edwardsville. She had decided to begin teaching to help pay for a horse that she loved. Built in 1918, the old high school that felt enormous to me as a child still stands at the corner of Third and Cedar Streets. It looks like many public institutions in the area with a red brick façade on a limestone foundation.

More than three thousand people lived in town, many of them black, and it was during the height of desegregation. Mom's classroom was in the school basement, and it was her first experience interacting with African Americans. She taught special education and English, and her classes included almost every black student on campus. She immersed herself in their lives and counseled students eagerly. Before long, rumors circulated about the pastor's wife and her fondness for black students.

Mom picked me up from school every afternoon. Rather than going home, we often set out on counseling excursions. During one of these trips, I followed Mom through a cinder block house without electricity. Kerosene lanterns threw flickering light across dirt floors in the pitch dark. Six children lived inside and shared a single bed. There were three or four beds in one bedroom, all crammed together. The youngest, a baby, screamed when we arrived. I looked into the crib and saw that the child's hair was all gone. The older kids also had bald spots, where their skin had turned white.

Mom lifted the child close and patted its back until it quieted. As she did, I looked toward a dim corner of the room. Lots of little eyes stared back at me. The high-pitched squeal of rats sent chills through my body. Looking up, I saw blood seeping from the baby's scalp. On the way home, Mom told me the rats had eaten the child's hair.

Many of the black families in eastern Kansas descended from tenant farmers, who had descended from slaves. Although Kansas was never a slave state, it played a dominant role in events leading up to the Civil War. Following the Kansas-Nebraska Act of 1854, pro- and anti-slavery supporters rushed into Kansas in hopes of influencing its stance on slavery. On January 29, 1861, Kansas entered the Union as a free state. Less than three months later, the Civil War began.

Despite its anti-slavery history, the Kansas community of my youth nourished racial prejudice. It seemed as if there was only one exception to this, and it was Sydney Lou. Mom never cared where people came from or how they looked. She only cared about helping them.

I remember one student in particular from her first year at Bonner Springs High. His name was Silas, and he was black. Silas was the son of a single mother, and they lived above the tavern that she operated. He was gregarious and well known at school and around Bonner Springs. The year Silas left Bonner Springs High, the local newspaper ran photos of every graduating senior and a short description of their post-high school plans. Under Silas' name it reads: "My future plans are attending Phillips University in Enid, Oklahoma. I plan to major in Social Studies."

Silas was one of many black students Mom led to Phillips. Grandpa Hughes helped by offering small scholarships. The application process was simple: Mom told Grandpa about the students, and Grandpa agreed to help pay their way. During Mom's own time at Phillips, she had watched proudly as the university enrolled its first two black students. School segregation was ending throughout the South, and Mom and Dad had a front-row seat to the change.

School integration also affected me. In Edwardsville, I was one of the few white students to attend an interracial elementary school with black and white students. As I moved through first grade, Mom often talked about the importance of treating all people equally. Dad delivered sermons on similar topics and wrote a column about family, religion, and sometimes race for the local newspaper. From the front pew of Edwardsville Christian Church, Mom and I listened carefully as he spoke.

Mom and I also began to escape across the Kansas River more and more to see Grandma and Grandpa Hughes. We spent most Saturdays with them in Claycomo. Grandma and Grandpa's farm became our refuge from home. On the same acreage where Mom grew up,

I ran free. Ricky and Patty became my best friends. Ricky and Patty were two of the children who were left for dead by their parents. When my grandparents were asked to come and see these children, their heads were full of lice and they cried from hunger. Whitey and Pauline took Ricky and Patty, the youngest two, home with them. The older children were taken by other members of the community.

"Do you want to go to Grandma and Grandpa's house?" were my favorite words to hear.

It was about an hour from Bonner Springs, Kansas to Claycomo, Missouri. But this was a safe haven. We rode horses, jumped on a giant trampoline, and made huge forts from hay bales in the barn. We'd play for hours until Grandma called us for dinner. On the best days, she served hamburgers, shakes, and fries from a nearby burger joint.

My grandparents knew about the abuse. The first time my dad hit my mom she was sitting on a toilet seat, eight months pregnant with me. He smacked her so hard that he knocked her off the seat. She told both sets of parents at the time, and they had a conversation with Dad. But they also asked Mom what she had done to provoke him. So while the farm was a sanctuary for us, my grandparents ignored the real reason we were there so often. It was never discussed.

Making a Personal Connection to the Global Goals

For me, sharing my story with others and the influence my upbringing has had on why I care about the global goals has made them more personal. Recounting my story to different audiences has made me realize that we all have a story to tell and these goals are not just about the larger world—they are about each of us realizing our full potential as human beings and understanding the ways that we can be intimately connected to the goals through our own stories.

Throughout the years at dinner parties, meetings, prayer groups, and small gatherings of friends and strangers, whenever I was invited to tell my story, I was always amazed at how people responded and wanted to know more about how my childhood has shaped the work I do today. So I began writing . . . not knowing where it would lead. More recently, I have been bold and taken the risk of sharing my story with larger audiences. The impact the story had on three distinct groups of people has been part of my own journey of "Making the Global Goals Personal." It has led me to want to be a "game changer," an agent for positive change in the world.

The first audience I shared my story with was within my own organization. Global Impact is comprised of sixty-plus staff, predominantly young professional millennials, Gen Xers, and a few late baby boomers who have come together to grow global philanthropy, build partnerships and resources, and raise the visibility of global issues that affect the world's most vulnerable people. They deem themselves "change agents," "global citizens," and "game changers" who working together make an impact through partnerships committed to the Global Goals. How we got there is in large part because we have shared our stories.

At an all-staff conference, Ann Canela, Global Impact's Vice President, colleague, and friend, challenged all of us to tell our personal stories as part of a storytelling workshop. The art or practice of storytelling is about telling the story of self, the story of us, and the story of others. Our own personal stories should and do influence what we choose to do with the life we have been given and how our lives can be used to impact others. Ann asked me to model for everyone and share my story first so that the rest of the Global Impact staff would be comfortable sharing their stories.

I shared how as a child the abuse of my mother, the poverty of those who lived on the other side of the tracks in Edwardsville, Kansas, and the faces of the black families and children who were most impacted by poverty and prejudice have helped me understand the difference between rich and poor.

After telling my story, we all shed tears. Then we heard the next story and the next—all equally poignant and personal journeys about how each of us had come to be together at Global Impact in that moment in time. It was a personal transformation we all shared. Since then, staff have taken on their own "connecting to mission" initiative, engaging each other, our board of directors, and our partners in sharing their stories to learn about global issues, such as child trafficking, gender violence and inequality, and the issues of securing water and sanitation and a safe food supply. We have had a local food drive, packed food stuffs and sanitation kits for the homeless, watched movies, had presentations to learn about the work of our charity partners, and erected mosquito nets over our work cubicles to learn more about malaria prevention.

We have even had "Lola the Chicken" visit the office to understand the importance of livestock for families around the world in their effort to have a source for their food for years to come. Now that we have completed the Connecting to Mission series, the staff has launched a new initiative to learn about the Global Goals for Sustainable Development through the lens of Global Goal #17—Partnerships—and the role of Global Impact. The team even reengineered games and created a global goals song list to educate each other as global citizens and celebrate the goals.

The second audience I shared my story with was a much different one—the US Department of Defense at the Defense Intelligence Complex based in Washington, DC, across the Potomac River from Global Impact's offices and Center for Growing Global Philanthropy. The Defense Intelligence Agency (DIA) invited me to be the featured speaker for the kick-off of their national 2015 Combined Federal Campaign. The day of the kick-off, I made my way in the pouring rain and severe winds to a facility I didn't even know existed. After the long process of getting through security, I was escorted to a large auditorium.

I entered the auditorium and was surprised to see close to 800 men and women who have dedicated their service to keeping America safe. I was introduced by an African American two-star general with his own story of sacrifice and service around the world for his country. The podium was only a few steps from the front row, but it seemed like it took forever to make my way toward it. I looked out to the audience and began to tell my story. I told them about the abuse of my mom, and how Jefferson, Mom, and I had to leave the country because of the prejudice towards an interracial family. I shared how there were kids like me all over the world and that each of us has an opportunity to help them realize their potential.

Then I recounted a recent visit I had to the US headquarters for Doctors Without Borders (MSF). I explained that their staff told me how important the contributions are that they receive from federal employees through what is called the Combined Federal Campaign because they are able to use those dollars where most needed. Then I recognized a series of names and staff pictures at the front of the room with messages from their colleagues. These were staff being held hostage around the world because of their service to others. The funds raised by federal employees were helping Doctors Without Borders (MSF) in their efforts to gain the freedom of their fellow workers and return them to their families.

I thanked the men and women in the auditorium for what they did every day and for their campaign contributions, as an extension of who they are and their commitment to public service.

Not long after this, I shared my story with a third and completely different audience. I had been invited to speak in New York to a group of corporate executives responsible for corporate social responsibility inside their respective Fortune 500 companies. The topic was on the role the private sector can play to achieve the Global Goals. That same week I would be participating in a United Nations launch of Impact 2030, a private sector volunteer engagement initiative for which Global Impact has the privilege to serve as secretariat and fiscal agent.

I began my panel presentation by emphasizing that without the private sector involvement, the Goals would not be achieved. I revealed ways in which the private sector could contribute by raising resources, creating business solutions, and providing skill-based volunteers to support the work of the Global Goals around the world.

Then I shared my story and explained that for me it made the Goals "personal," meaning I understood that I had a strong connection to them because of my own experience. They were not just something for the "other" person out there whose experience and situation across the globe was vastly different from mine. I then encouraged each person in the room to think about how their story connected them to this work if they were to fully understand the role they must play to change the world. Afterward, you could have heard a pin drop. A number of participants went out of their way to thank me for being willing to share. I realized what an impact my story had in making the Global Goals personal.

It was emotionally moving for me to realize that divulging my personal story and why I cared about the Global Goals had meaning for others, which is why I will be sharing it with you throughout this book. As you read about the various critical issues that challenge our world today—from abuse to hunger to prejudice—I will then use my story as a way to make these problems more personal and to reveal to you that many of these global issues are also right here at home. . . .

THE GLOBAL GOALS
For Sustainable Development

CHAPTER TWO

Take Me with You

During the summer of 1964 racial tensions erupted in America. That July, President Lyndon Johnson signed the Civil Rights Act. Less than a year earlier JFK was assassinated. In Claycomo, I watched the president's funeral on my grandparent's color television. Soon afterward Dad supported efforts to form a local interracial ministerial alliance. One of the group's other members preached at Gethsemane Baptist, a black church just two miles from our own.

Mom, Dad, and I visited Gethsemane together. When we arrived, the Reverend Jefferson Jackson stood outside. Jefferson and my dad were the first two co-chairs of the Black and White Ministerial Alliance. His small church was plastered in white stucco, and a white brick extension was under construction. The buildings rose from an otherwise empty field north of town. In the morning light, a white cross cast a long black shadow westward across the surrounding grass. Some of the church elders also stood outside. Like the Reverend, they wore dark suits, pressed white shirts, and thin dark ties.

Jefferson Jackson introduced the group with a firm handshake and a wide smile. He gave us a tour of the church grounds and the new construction that was being completed by church volunteers, cinder block by cinder block, and he led us inside to the front pew. Behind us, the rows of the sanctuary began to fill quickly. Almost all the men wore suits. The women wore long dresses, gloves, and hats. Mom recognized some of her students from school.

Gethsemane Church in 2012

Pastor Jefferson Jackson

Soon the building seemed to bulge. I couldn't believe how many people fit inside. My biggest surprise was yet to come. In a storm of energy and music, the choir exploded from behind a red curtain near the pulpit. Its members clapped and sang in unison as the congregation burst into song. Then, one by one, the elders stepped out. Music filled my body. Goose bumps spread across my arms. Suddenly, at a perfect crescendo of energy, the Reverend Jackson appeared in front of the church.

"Sing it, everyone!" he shouted.

The building pulsed. The reverend's voice carried with more grace and beauty than I had ever heard. His deep baritone sent vibrations through my body. I stood up, stunned. The man in front of me was a preacher unlike any I'd ever seen. He exuded electricity you could feel. That morning's service had the spark and flash of a lightning strike.

Jefferson Jackson was a handsome man of not quite six feet. He had loosely curled hair and a muscular frame built through years of manual labor. His smile was as broad as the Kansas River and just as easy. Jefferson was born in Bristow, Oklahoma, in the spring of 1922. His twin sister died at birth. All told, Jefferson's parents raised eight children—five boys and three girls.

Jefferson's dad was the son of a sharecropper and the first member of his family to own land. Jefferson grew up in a two-room house without running water or electricity. The girls slept in one bed and the boys in another. Family meals often included biscuits, bean lard, and grits. Jefferson would later recall how special those few times were each year when his mom put meat on the table.

Jefferson went barefoot for much of his childhood. Each afternoon after school, he worked in the fields with his siblings. By fourth grade, he nearly dropped out of school. His teacher convinced him to stay by giving him his first pair of shoes, and Jefferson managed to remain in school through tenth grade. He was later drafted into World War II. That same night, he fell to his knees and prayed. If God didn't send him to war, Jefferson promised to dedicate his life to serving the church.

Jefferson served in the military but was spared from being deployed overseas. Following his time in the service, he struggled to find work in Kansas City. Young, undereducated, and poor, he thought back on the day he was drafted. On a starry night, Jefferson walked outside alone and looked up.

"If you want me to serve you, send me a sign," he said. "Rattle the heavens!"

At that exact moment, a single shooting star left a fiery trail across the night sky.

Jefferson never looked back. He joined a gospel quartet and began taking ministry classes. He struggled to read and write, but he could read the Bible cover to cover. He paid his bills by working in the vast stockyards of Kansas City. Later, he picked up a warehouse job working nights. Along the way, he married a spirited woman everyone called Lulu. She loved outrageous hats almost as much as she loved sleeping around. Despite the cheating, Jefferson stayed. Lulu loved Jefferson for one reason: Their marriage made her the first lady at Gethsemane Baptist.

During our second visit to Gethsemane, Mom and I sat next to Lulu. Through the ministerial alliance, Jefferson had invited Dad to preach. That Sunday, Dad told a story from the book of Matthew. In it, a frenzied crowd surrounds Jesus as he heals two blind men. Dad used the story to talk about forgiveness and new life. It was a beautiful message . . . but it wasn't real. When his sermon ended, I looked at Mom. Tears poured from her eyes.

Mom's work helping black students took a dramatic turn during my second year of school when she began mentoring Michael, a freshman in her last class of the day. One of six children, Michael lived in the black section of Bonner Springs. He was fourteen years old and one of the smallest freshmen in his class. After school, Michael often lingered in Mom's classroom. He'd sit quietly reading or doing homework. Eventually Mom offered him a ride home. When they arrived at his house, Mom saw Michael's dad unconscious in the dirt yard. Stepping over him, she followed Michael inside, met his mom, and left.

Back at school, Michael began to confide in Mom about his family. Sitting in her classroom long after the final bell, he painted a dismal picture of life at home. His dad was perpetually drunk and usually violent. His mom seemed forever detached, like the walking dead. Mom felt deeply troubled by the stories Michael shared with her and desperately wanted to protect him from this disturbing environment.

Eventually, Mom and I drove together to Michael's house. As we pulled up, I saw him sitting on the front step. He smiled as we walked toward him.

"Sydney, what are you doing here?" Michael asked.

"I'm here to take you home with us, where you'll be safe," Mom replied.

As we spoke, his mother appeared on the porch. Mom told her matter-of-factly that Michael was coming to live with us.

Michael's mom stared at her blankly and said, "Go on, Michael, go with them." She nodded and walked back inside. Michael never would have survived in that house. He was far too different from his tough siblings, who ultimately wound up in jail.

At the parsonage, we set up a cot in the laundry room. Michael became so used to the sound of the washer and dryer that he preferred to sleep with them running. They also muffled the sounds of Dad's abuse. Michael never upset Dad—he did his chores and never talked back. When Dad hit Mom, Michael disappeared silently.

Scott's "brother" Michael

I looked up to Michael from the start. He was twice my age, and he dressed with a flare otherwise unseen in Edwardsville. I grew to love Michael as my brother. He helped me feel safe when our house turned violent. He would try to distract me during a fight, taking me on excursions in the car. We would flee to the grocery store or the high school, or our favorite escape—shopping for clothes.

By 1966 Dad's abuse was no longer a family secret. While most of my mom's bruises weren't outwardly visible, elders in the church became aware of the situation because she often sought protection in other houses down the street. At Edwardsville Christian, rumors about Mom and her students also spread. That spring, after almost eight years, Dad lost his pastorship. While he searched for a new position, Dad, Mom, Michael, and I stayed with Grandma and Grandpa Hughes. We joined Dad for a couple of family job interviews. On one Sunday, he delivered a guest sermon at a large church in an affluent area of Kansas City. Michael joined us near the front of the all-white congregation. We were never asked to return.

Dad eventually took over as director of Tall Oaks, a Christian camp and conference center west of Bonner Springs. It occupied a few hundred acres along the north bank of the Kansas River. The day we moved in, I fell in love with the place. Huge oak trees shaded the property and turned a rusty orange each fall. Scattered throughout, broad meadows and bunkhouses welcomed visitors year-round, especially in summer. A single-lane gravel road meandered through the grounds, passing the dining hall, cabins, a pool with two diving boards, and a large open-air A-frame shelter that served as a chapel. At the end of the road, a rugged bluff grew thick with oak trees and angled steeply toward the river.

The camp director's house felt like a mansion compared to the parsonage. With a family room, a formal living room, large kitchen, three bedrooms, two bathrooms, a double-car garage, and a basement, it made the parsonage look like a cage. For the first time in his life, Michael had his own bedroom.

At Tall Oaks, I often walked through the woods alone and explored the places few campers ever saw. I hiked game trails and made a few of my own. But my favorite activity was sitting in the midst of the oak trees, high on the bluff, and looking south over the railroad tracks and river. Sandbars and deep green thickets dotted the river's course. During fall and winter, after the leaves fell, you could see the water pass slowly below and watch trains roll west toward Lawrence or east toward the small town of De Soto and beyond there to Bonner Springs and Edwardsville. At the top of the bluff, the trains sounded soft and faint, not at all like they had for so many years when living right next to the tracks.

About the time we moved to Tall Oaks, Mom bought thirty-five acres on the outskirts of Edwardsville. Grandma and Grandpa lent her the money and helped us build a small barn with a tack house. Shortly afterward, Grandpa drove us across the river to an Arabian horse farm in De Soto. I fell in love with a black colt named Midnight. Grandpa bought him for me, and we eventually kept four horses on the property.

Back at Tall Oaks, we quickly established a family routine. Each morning Mom and Michael drove to Bonner Springs while Dad and I ate breakfast. Mom continued to teach at the high school, and Michael became heavily involved with school activities. He acted in plays, made the honor roll, and led the band as drum major. As a senior, he was pictured on eight pages of the school yearbook, more than almost anyone else.

While Michael flourished, my relationship with my father disintegrated. In Edwardsville, Dad and I had rarely spent time alone. Now, each morning over cereal and toast, the barrier between us was stripped raw. The gaps in our relationship became chasms. I wasn't interested in anything he did, and he cared little about me. I think Dad saw me as an adversary rather than a son. During the long silences that hung over breakfast, I felt anger toward my father. I was angry with him for what he was and for what he wasn't, for what he did to my mom and for what he failed to do with me.

"Scottie, are you ready for school?" Dad asked one morning.

"Of course I'm ready for school!" I responded sullenly.

"Well, wash your dishes," he said. Everything always had to be perfectly in order.

"I *always* wash my dish," I replied with a bit of attitude.

"Don't you know not to talk like that to your father?" Dad shouted through gritted teeth.

Inevitably, something I said always struck him the wrong way. I hated those moments.

After breakfast, Dad drove me two miles to Linwood Elementary School. Fewer than five hundred people lived in town. If nothing else, Linwood was poor. A small post office accounted for most of the town activity. When Dad didn't drive me to school, I caught the bus at the end of the camp road or drove in with Slim, the camp handyman. Slim was white, skinny, and tall. I remember his presence standing in stark contrast to Dad, who by then weighed much more than he did during his college years. Slim obeyed Dad without question and quickly became his most trusted employee.

On Sundays, our family attended church a few blocks from the University of Kansas in Lawrence. Afterward, we returned straight home. Dad worked in his office and Mom read the newspaper in the living room. While Michael caught up on homework, I played war with little pretend plastic soldiers made of dominoes and Lincoln Logs. I would often stop playing and check on my mom to make sure she was okay.

On one of these Sundays, I went to check on Mom. I was watching from the next room when Dad approached her from behind. He lifted his hands and began to rub her shoulders. Then he curled his fingers around her throat and began to squeeze. I froze. I could see Mom convulse and the color drain from her face. From my hiding spot in the next room, I watched in what seemed like slow motion as Mom coughed and grabbed her throat in desperation. Then, just as quickly as it had begun, Dad released his grip and walked away.

Each night as I fell asleep, I wondered if he'd hit her before morning. My nightmares became reality. I'd wake to the sound of screaming or of Dad pounding on the bathroom door. On the worst nights, I could hear Dad hitting her, followed by whimpers of pain and tears. Through it all, Mom kept working, even when I woke to the sound of the front door slamming and gravel crunching in the driveway, as she sped away into the night.

I once tried to stop Dad from hurting Mom. I was in bed when the noise began. When I heard the bathroom door slam, I got up. Dad turned in the hallway to find me staring at him.

"Go back to your room," he said, looking down at me. "Your mother locked herself in the bathroom again. I can't stop her. All I want to do is stop her from hurting herself. She's crazy. You know that."

I could hear Mom crying on the other side of the door. I spoke in my loudest voice.

"Mom, are you okay? Can you come out? Can you tell me you're okay?"

The bathroom door swung open and Mom rushed out wearing her nightgown.

"I'm okay," she said. "Go back to bed. He won't hurt you."

She ran down the hall, grabbed her keys and purse, and started for the front door. Dad tried to follow her, but I stepped in front of him. He stopped. It was all the time Mom needed.

My greatest fear as a child was that my mom would leave and not take me with her—those nights when she would run past, bare-foot out the door, I would put my head through the curtains against the window to see her drive off in her Volkswagen bug, knowing she was finally safe that night. She would reappear early the next morning in time to get ready for school and drive away again to escape to the safety of the classroom and work. But I feared that one day she would not return . . . and I would be left behind.

By night, my mom was a tortured and battered housewife. By day, Sydney Lou was a high school English teacher for special needs students, a pastor's wife, and a community activist. She was also a faithful friend, an accomplished piano player, and a creative artist. Sydney Lou showed Tennessee walking horses, mentored troubled kids, produced church plays and pageants, made murals for the school and church, and spent long hours consoling friends in need. Whether doing this was to get away or to express compassion to others and feel self-worth, she would go and I would accompany her. Sometimes, we just went to a movie or drove to Grandpa and Grandma's house—the ultimate retreat. When Mom said, "Do you want to go with me?" I would always reply with great conviction, "Take me with you," and I was out the door and in the passenger seat of the Volkswagen before she could change her mind.

There are only a few days from around this time that I look back on fondly, mainly the days when Mom and I played hooky from school. Without Dad knowing, one hot day in late spring we took off toward Edwardsville, turned north across the railroad tracks, and drove along a series of one-lane roads. On the way, we saw livestock and tiny homes on tiny farms. Many of the buildings were in disrepair. We turned down a dirt road, drove past a rundown house, and stopped in front of a pigpen and a large chicken coop. Looking around, I saw an old emerald green Ford truck. Nearby, a black man wearing overalls and a straw hat walked toward us.

The first feature I recognized about the Reverend Jefferson Jackson was his smile. Mom explained that she and Jefferson had become friends since our visits to Gethsemane Baptist, as Jefferson showed us around the small plot of land he had rented where he could grow some vegetables, have a chicken coop, and keep his pigs. While we strolled around the property, he spoke about how he had raised animals and worked on a farm since he was a kid. I remember the smell of pigs rolling in the mud.

"Here, take this bucket and try to get it over the fence," Jefferson said, including me as he fed the pigs. "Take this cabbage."

"Jefferson, this pig is going to eat my hand!" I yelled in delight.

"Boy, that pig's not going to eat your hand," he laughed good-naturedly.

After a while, the three of us jumped into Jefferson's green truck. We drove along more dirt roads and eventually parked by a large pond, behind a line of cars. For the rest of the day, I caught more carp than I could count. Jefferson taught me how to roll giant stinky globs of cornmeal into bait balls and make them stick to the hook. There must have been thousands of fish in that pond. Wherever I looked, people were reeling them in. Along the entire shore, Mom and I were the only white people.

The places we would go to escape weren't always so secret. Mom's passion and commitment to her beloved horse "Lady in Silver" was one such diversion. She had spent a good portion of her meager teacher's salary, $10,000, to buy Lady in Silver, a pure white Tennessee Walking Horse for show. Lady in Silver was trained and boarded outside of Kansas City. One summer, we drove the long distance four days a week so that Mom could train and ride Lady in Silver. Every weekend, we met the trainer and the horse at a competition or show. Mom was amazing to watch on that horse. She would dye her hair at the beauty parlor a different color every week to match her outfit—red, lavender, pink, black, and silver. The two of them would then light up the show ring with a sea of sequins. The kids at school always wondered what color hair she would have each week. After fourteen 1st place ribbons, Mom and Lady in Silver entered and won 4th place in the American Royal. Her hair fell out at the end of the show season from all that bleaching, but it was glorious while it lasted. We would both have a passion for horses for many years to come.

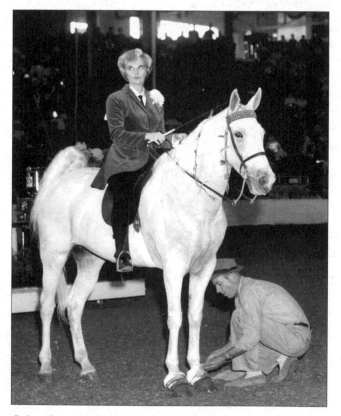

Sydney Lou with Lady in Silver

In April 1968 I was ten years old. I didn't know much about Martin Luther King Jr. I knew he was a civil rights leader, and I knew he was a pastor. That second part resonated most with me. When I heard the news about King's assassination, I remember thinking how Dad and King had something in common. I also thought about Jefferson. I wondered if other black pastors would be shot.

Mom had been at school when it happened. She still taught most of the black students in the high school, either in her special education or regular English classes. After the news spread, the principal announced over the loud speaker that all the Negro students could go home for the day. Mom immediately rushed out of her classroom to the administrative office to protest. She believed the high school was giving the wrong message by treating the white students different from the black students. Sending only the black students home could cause even more of a racial divide and social unrest, she argued. The principal finally agreed with Mom, and all students were then given the option to leave school for the rest of the day.

Less than twenty-four hours after King's shooting, hundreds of high school and college students marched in downtown Kansas City. City officials assigned every black officer they had to help control the crowd. For a week, Mom and Dad read the newspaper anxiously. People all around the country feared riots. At home, we watched television broadcasts of the violence in Chicago and Washington, DC. Towns across the rest of America grew restive. But many remained calm, including ours.

Two months after King's assassination, one early spring day, Mom unexpectedly picked me up from school. Linwood was a lot closer to Tall Oaks where we lived and my dad worked. Mom commuted each day some thirty miles on her trip back and forth Bonner Springs High School, so it was a big surprise when she arrived to take me home.

"I have something to tell you, and I needed you to hear it from me," she said, as we drove home in the car. "Dad and I are getting a divorce. I have told him I don't want anything from him—except you. You can still visit your dad but you will live with me. We will be moving as soon as the school year is over, back to Edwardsville. We will live on the farm property there. So I need to know," she said, "are you okay with all this?"

At first, I didn't know what to say. Thoughts and questions as jumbled as a sunflower field after the harvest flooded my brain. Then a sense of relief and joy overcame me. No longer would I live in fear. I began to rattle off questions.

"What did he say to you when you told him you were leaving?" I asked.

"Well, he wasn't happy about it, but he also wasn't sad because I think he wanted to get rid of me."

"What about me? Did he want me, too?" I asked.

That last question stuck. We had been driving aimlessly around Linwood. Mom pulled over, stopped the car, and looked at me. "More important," she said, "is that I want you. I told him that I would not take any money from him if I could have full custody and take you. And he said fine."

"What about furniture?"

"We'll take Grandpa's furniture."

"Where will we live?"

"We'll get a mobile home and put it on the farm. If you don't want to go, I understand."

"Well, you're not gonna leave me, are you?" I asked desperately.

"No, of course not," Mom replied.

"You have to take me with you. You can't leave me. You have to take me with you," I pleaded.

Michael left for Phillips University that summer. Grandpa Hughes paid his way. Not long after he moved out, we'd gone to the farm to check on the animals, and Michael told Mom he needed to speak to her. They sat in the car until it grew dark and talked for a long time while I waited outside.

"Sydney, I have something I have to tell you," he said. "I have feelings for other men."

"Why did you want to tell me?" Mom asked.

"Because," he said, "I knew you'd still love me."

Michael was a talented young man who was ostracized from his family and from his peers in school. He would eventually die of HIV AIDS before there was a known treatment. We kept in touch and visited over the years, and even had dinner with Michael and his partner. But we had no idea how sick he was.

Mom and I moved to the farm near Edwardsville. She bought a doublewide aluminum trailer that was white with a silver roof and parked it next to the barn. Mom transformed the tack room of the barn into our living room, which was now conveniently attached to the trailer to expand our humble living space. Grandma and Grandpa Hughes provided fancy new furniture that rested on the dark turquoise indoor/outdoor carpeting covering the concrete slab. We embraced our new lives on the farm and used our acreage to grow a variety of vegetables and raise animals, who often wound up eating the tomatoes, lettuce, radishes, and squash.

Along with our horses, we kept seven pigs and a goat. One of our pigs had a hole in his side, with a colostomy bag hanging down. We also had four cats, two dogs, and a guinea pig. My dog Dewey had passed away by then; someone had poisoned him. On hot days, the horses shaded themselves under large persimmon trees that grew near the fence line. During long summer nights, sunsets turned the farm golden while warm winds blew across the sloping fields.

To my chagrin, Mom made sure we brought the piano with the chipped ivory keys with us and placed it prominently in the living

Sydney feeding her pet pig

room. For as long as I can remember, my mother made me take piano lessons. At first I wanted to, but then it was always time for me to come inside to practice the piano while the other kids got to stay outside and play. I never played very well. I had enough of an ear for it, but I didn't put the time into learning how to read music easily. After we moved into the trailer on the farm, Mom made me start piano lessons again. In the summer months the tack room with the concrete floor underneath remained cool. But in the winter, it was cold and there was no way to get warm with just the electric portable wall heater. Nonetheless, I would bundle up and try to concentrate enough to at least pretend to be practicing.

One day after school while pretending to practice, I started to think about Mom and all she had sacrificed for me, and I wrote a song for her. It went something like this:

My mother used to sit me on her lap.

She would read me the stories of the Bible.

I would love to hear them so very much.

Now I know, Lord, Now I know, Lord, that someday you'll come for me.

When that Day comes, when that day comes, Lord,
the angels will sing out in heaven, and the heavens
will open for you and for me.

On that day, Lord, my mother and I will be free.

Shortly after leaving Tall Oaks, Mom and I became the first white members of Gethsemane Baptist. We also began to see much more of Jefferson. He often drove by the farm, and sometimes he and Mom sat outside until dusk. I watched them from inside the trailer. By fall of 1968, my parent's divorce became official. Soon afterward Jefferson spent the night, and he and Mom lived together unmarried.

I began fifth grade. I did well in school, which caused some jealousy among the other students. It was the early days of integration, and the majority of the students in our school were black. One day at recess some of the black boys began taunting me because they knew about Mom and Jefferson.

I had come out into the hall to wait in line for the water fountain. The bathroom nearby had two entrances—one from inside the hall and another that led outside to the playground, volleyball courts, and a large field. When I finished taking a drink, I entered the bathroom to head outside and a few of the boys stopped me.

"I know that your mom and Jefferson are together. Thanks a lot for ruining our church," one of them said.

"Boy, your mom sure did create a mess," said another one.

"Well, that's the way it goes," said the first boy. "These white women can't keep away from a black stud."

"She didn't try to ruin your church," I argued. "You don't know what you're talking about!"

"Well, she was just looking for a black stud."

"You better watch your mouth!"

"I don't need to watch my mouth. Your mom's a n-gger lover."

My fists reacted before my brain. I hit him and he hit back. I hit him again and then started to run, but both boys pulled me down on the ground in a tug of war.

A few minutes later, I sat in the principal's office. My lip was bleeding badly and tears streamed down my face. When I got home, I told Mom what had happened. She looked sad. Then she made sure my butt hurt, too. Fighting wasn't allowed—period.

"No matter what they say to you, you can't respond," she said. "You have to be bigger than that."

Dad also had issues with Mom dating Jefferson. He picked me up from the farm every other weekend, and he asked lots of questions about them, about what they did and if Jefferson spent the night. One time, Dad arrived and knocked on the door, wanting to come in, rather than leaving right away like we usually did.

"I just want to come in for a bit," he said.

"Why?" I asked.

"I just want to look around and see that you're safe."

"I'm safe," I replied as he began to walk into the bedrooms.

"Why are you in my mom's room?" I asked. He went into the bathroom and started counting the toothbrushes. "You're not supposed to do this," I continued.

"It looks like someone else is living here," he said.

"That's none of your business," I said angrily.

Once we arrived at Tall Oaks, I went straight to my bedroom.

Dad came in and said, "Maybe we'll go to a hockey game this weekend."

"That sounds good," I said. "I've never been to a hockey game."

"I want to talk to you about something first," Dad said seriously. "You and your mom are living with a black man in sin. I want to get you out of this situation."

"I don't need to be out of it," I argued.

"Your mom has lots of issues and likes black men," he kept on.

"You don't know what the hell you're talking about!" I yelled. "You beat her for years! I don't want to go anywhere with you. Get out. Get out!"

I insisted he take me home the next morning. It was the first time I realized he was humiliated by the situation. It wasn't about me or my safety; it was solely about the fact that it was embarrassing to him. Somewhere deep down I began to understand that he was going to cause trouble for me.

My visits with Dad almost always ended badly. He bad-mouthed Mom constantly. He said she had a *thing* for black men. He accused her of visiting students at Phillips University and of cheating on him during their marriage.

He also spoke badly of Jefferson. "Do you really want to live with . . . " he'd pause, drawing out the final two words, *"Black people?"*

I never understood where Dad's hatred began. My dad's father told my mom that it was because my dad used to see him beat his own wife, my dad's mother. In Edwardsville, Dad worked hard to help the races find common ground. That's how we'd met Jefferson in the first place. He even wrote a regular newspaper column on religion, often covering race relations and the importance of breaking the color barriers that defined so many churches. Years later, no matter how hard I tried to give Dad the benefit of the doubt, I never could. He'd either been a racist in disguise all along or turned into one when Mom fell in love with Jefferson. Either way, his feelings ripped an even greater divide between us.

Less than a year after the divorce, Mom lost her job at Bonner Springs High. The principal told her she might be happier if she left. He didn't need to say anything else. By being together, Mom and Jefferson challenged people's accepted boundaries. They were the only mixed-race couple most people knew. When students and faculty began to gossip about the white teacher and the black preacher, Mom's days at Bonner Springs High were done.

Jefferson also left Gethsemane Baptist. He kept his day job working in a warehouse for a sporting goods company in Kansas City. Not long after he and Mom began seeing each other, Jefferson gave me a basketball and nailed up a hoop at the farm. We often shot baskets together until it was too dark to see. That ball became my new best friend.

Jefferson had a mean hook shot and he would laugh and say, "Boy, you can't shoot." Then I would shoot and make a basket and get ahead of him, and we'd laugh. He never gritted his teeth or said a bad word about anyone, in contrast to my real dad, who always had something nasty to say. During these times, I realized that you could have happy moments, that there was such a thing as family. A man's role didn't have to revolve only around being the disciplinarian. You didn't have to fear a father figure.

Mom found a new job teaching high school equivalency courses in Kansas City. She also tried to get me to join an all-black Boy Scout troop. During my first meeting, one of the older boys made me stand on my head against a wall the entire time. I never went back.

It took Jefferson's first wife almost two years to sign her divorce papers. Soon afterward, he and Mom spent a weekend in Nebraska. When they returned, they were married. It was still not accepted for an interracial couple to be married in Kansas. As a wedding gift, Jefferson gave Mom a white miniature poodle she named Trixie.

A few months after their marriage, the three of us took a day trip through the Kansas countryside. We spent hours driving through the hills and over long flat expanses, finding places none of us had seen before. It was a perfect day. When we returned home, we saw a narrow column of smoke rising near the farm. Jefferson skidded to a stop in front of our gate. Looking out the truck window, I saw a small wooden cross smoldering in a pile of ashes.

"What is it, a cross?" I asked.

Jefferson replied, "Boy, we don't know. Don't worry about it."

"Who would put something like that there? Why would they set a fire next to our driveway?"

Jefferson got out of the pickup to open the farm gate. When he got back to the car, he said, "Someone who just doesn't know any better. You just have to never mind people like that."

It was one more reminder that we were different and not accepted. It was interesting how quickly people thought the same thoughts about me and my mom that they thought about Jefferson because of his skin color. That burning cross was aimed at all three of us. I didn't escape it.

Dad filed for custody of me. In court, he claimed Mom wasn't fit to raise me. The judge made vague references to Mom's associations with "black people" and called her out for marrying Jefferson, who he referred to as "a Negro."

One weekend around this time, Dad drove to Missouri to pick me up from my grandparents' house. Mom told me to hide in the attic with Ricky and Patty. We turned off the lights and tried not to make any noise. Dad came to the front door and knocked. When no one answered, he moved to the side door and knocked again. Then he yelled my name and pounded on the door. Upstairs, I pressed myself flat on the floor and breathed slowly. I knew Dad could break down the door easily. I heard him walk across the driveway back toward his car. As he sped away, I looked out the attic window and saw him circling the block. He parked in front of the furniture store and went inside. He found Mom and started yelling. Jefferson was there and told him to calm down. Grandpa pulled down a horsewhip from a wall and chased Dad off the property.

Dad's attorney called the next day. Two lawyers watched as Mom delivered me to Dad. At the end of the weekend, I went back to Mom. Soon I wouldn't have that choice.

Strong Women, Strong World™

Ten years ago, a close friend and colleague at World Vision, Kathryn Compton, asked me in my capacity as a Senior Executive for World Vision if I would sponsor a luncheon in New York to increase aware-ness of the plight of women and girls around the world. At that time, we wanted to focus on the impact HIV AIDS was having on women. I agreed, even though the world was only beginning to pay attention to the issues affecting women in the developing world. Today, Strong Women, Strong World™ is a thriving campaign, an empowerment movement of women of faith to raise resources and awareness of issues, such as HIV AIDS, economic improvement, violence against women, child mar-riage, water and sanitation, maternal and newborn health, and girls' access to education.

I had the privilege in December 2015 of joining more than 200 women and men at the tenth annual Strong Women, Strong World™ gathering and luncheon. Global Impact was a proud sponsor.

Women account for more than 50 percent of the world's popula-tion, and yet they suffer disproportionately from domestic violence. How often does a man raise his voice or hand towards a woman because he can? Like my mother, women who are abused physically or even emotionally are led to believe it is somehow their fault. They fight back in their own way sometimes, taking even more abuse for the sake of their children.

One in four women will experience domestic violence in their life-time. Domestic violence is most likely to take place between 6:00 p.m. and 6:00 a.m. Domestic violence is the third leading cause of homeless-ness. More than four million women experience physical assault and/or verbal abuse by their partners. More than three million children witness domestic violence in their homes every year. Children are more likely to intervene when they witness severe violence against a parent, which can place a child at great risk of injury or even death.

The majority of human trafficking is of women and girls, and it is growing not diminishing around the world, with billions of dollars representing its not-so-underground industry. There were 4,168 human trafficking cases reported in 2015. Girl trafficking represents the majority of cases. 3,479 of the cases were against women and girls.

Every year more than fifteen million girls are married as children and denied their rights to health, education, and economic opportunity and robbed of their childhood. In rural Kenya I once witnessed with my own eyes the ceremony following the tradition of genital cutting of a twelve-year-old girl. She stood in the middle of the village for over a day as she waited to be betrothed to a man four times her age. As a result of this forced marriage, that little girl will never realize her full potential, and it is the rest of us who will miss out, not knowing what she could have really contributed to her family, her community, and the world.

Without access to family planning for women, other essential interventions to reduce poverty and inequality will be far less effective. Every year 300,000 women suffer a preventable death during pregnancy and childbirth. Women produce half the world's food but own or have legal rights to less than one percent of the land on which they produce that food. Two thirds of the children denied primary education are girls. Organizations like CARE, World Vision, Plan International, International Center for Research for Women (ICRW), and Landesa have made it their business to provide essential services for women and girls and break the cycle of poverty for half the world's population.

5 GENDER EQUALITY

GLOBAL GOAL 5

Gender Equality

Achieve gender equality and empower all women and girls

© David Snyder / CRW

In many developing nations, where girls are often valued less than boys, marrying daughters early can be viewed as a way to ease a family's financial burden. But for girls like Kasanesh, there is little benefit to this arrangement. Girls' childhood swiftly ends with the exchange of vows. Worldwide, most child brides drop out of school. Girl wives are more likely to experience domestic violence. Their mobility is restricted and they have little power in household decisions. In many countries, young brides often are at risk of a slew of health problems, including life-threatening complications from early pregnancy and childbirth.

Charities in Action

World Vision's Strong Women, Strong World™ initiative aims to empower, protect, educate, and nurture women and girls living in some of the most challenging places in the world

ICRW's research identifies women's contributions to their communities and the barriers—like HIV, violence, lack of education—that prevent them from being economically stable and able to fully participate in society.

CARE addresses gender inequality systematically by promoting girls' education and leadership, working with men and boys to change attitudes and perceptions, and addressing gender-based violence.

CHAPTER THREE

Leaving It All Behind

The night before my final custody decision, Mom and Jefferson drove me to Claycomo, Missouri. We had started the day in Lawrence, Kansas, where the court hearing was held. Earlier that day, the judge had refused to allow my testimony. Throughout the trial, he never asked me where I wanted to live, meaning with which parent. After the hearing, Mom and Jefferson met with our attorney, while I waited in the hall. More than an hour passed before they emerged. Mom's eyes were red.

In the parking lot, I sat between Mom and Jefferson on the bench seat of Jefferson's truck. As we drove away, Mom began to cry. Through her tears, I heard her say something.

"Scottie, we're going to lose you."

I was shocked. How could this be? I hadn't been allowed to tell the judge how scared I was of my dad, to tell him about all the abuse I had witnessed, about how Dad hit and choked Mom, about his anger, violence, and bigotry. Mom's worst news was yet to come.

"We might not get to see you at all," she said. "The judge doesn't think Jefferson and I should be married, and no one thinks you should be living with us, not even our own attorney. I'm sorry, Scottie. We tried."

I stared at the floor of the truck. Tears welled in my eyes. I didn't stop crying until I noticed Jefferson pass the turnoff to Edwardsville.

"We're going to Grandma and Grandpa's," Mom said.

When we arrived, Grandma gave me a huge hug. For dinner, Grandpa brought home my favorite milkshake, hamburgers, and fries. We ate and joked and laughed and tried not to think about what was coming. After we ate, we moved to the living room. Ricky and I sat together on a couch with overstuffed pillows. Across the room, Grandpa sat with the others and spoke quietly.

"You're going to lose tomorrow," he said. "If you don't show up, you'll be held in contempt. The only way to keep Scottie is to leave the country."

I couldn't believe what I was hearing. No one had said anything about this on the drive or during dinner. Looking across the room, I saw Grandpa's eyes. They looked sad.

"Then we'll just have to leave," Mom said. "We have no choice if we want to be together, and Jefferson and I can't leave Scottie behind."

Where would we go? Canada or Mexico seemed the most logical choices. Mom and I had been to Mexico before, but Jefferson had not. We all agreed that going south of the border for the three of us didn't make sense, because we knew there was just as much prejudice toward an interracial family there. We chose Canada. Mom had an aunt in Bremerton, Washington, near Vancouver, British Columbia, and Jefferson had a sister and family living outside of Seattle. We didn't know if we would be able to contact any of them. We would be on our own regardless of which country we sought refuge in. Grandpa Whitey would do what he could to help us, buying our tickets and giving us a wad of cash.

The rest of the night passed in a blur. We arrived back home very late and pulled out our suitcases. Jefferson went outside to feed the animals one last time. Mom told me to pack what I needed that could fit in one bag. I deflated my basketball as much as I could and packed it first. Next, I packed a set of dominos, some comic books, and a pair of drumsticks. In the little space that remained, I stuffed some clothes and a toothbrush and then fell asleep. Mom shook me awake before dawn. I could hear Jefferson down the hall. I took a quick shower, while he carried our suitcases out to the truck. Mom was the only one allowed to bring two bags. In her second, she packed Trixie. Just before we drove away, Jefferson handed me the key to the front door of the trailer.

"Go lock the door, Boy, and let's go," he said.

And we were gone.

Later that morning, as our flight lifted off, a judge's gavel fell in a half-empty courtroom. Somewhere beyond Kansas, I looked out a small oval window and watched the plains turn to rocky peaks, stabs of realization that we had, in the middle of a night that already seemed like a dream, packed our bags and run away. Behind us were the first twelve years of my life and the place I called home. We had left behind Dad, the evil lawyers, and a judge who wouldn't hear my story.

Hours later, looking out that same window, I saw only clouds. When they broke, snow-covered mountains filled the porthole. So did the tallest trees I had ever seen, sparkling water, and a city with skyscrapers that seemingly rose from the sea. Vancouver, British Columbia, stretched out below.

Fewer than twenty-four hours had passed since Grandma unfolded a partially torn road map on the living room coffee table and Grandpa placed his finger on a large dot in the upper left-hand corner. He'd visited the Northwest once before.

"It's beautiful country," he said. Now I knew what he meant.

A few days after we arrived, Mom called Grandpa from a payphone.

"They held you in contempt," he told her. "There's a court order demanding your return. They're going to charge you with kidnapping."

Mom hung up. It was April 1970.

In Vancouver, it hadn't taken long for Mom and Jefferson to discover that finding work would be nearly impossible. During our first dinner in the city, they listened carefully as our waitress, an immigrant from Hong Kong, described the detailed paperwork required to obtain work permits. The more she talked, the more they realized how unprepared we were to run away. Any paperwork would be too much for a family trying to hide.

The ferry from mainland Canada to Vancouver Island carried hundreds of passengers and cars. We planned to cross to the island and reenter the US on another ferry. If all went well, we'd slip back into the country at a little-known border crossing in the western reaches of Washington State.

As our second ferry steered south, we had no idea what, or who, was waiting for us on the other side. During the nearly four-hour crossing, Mom filled out our customs' sheets. She used Jefferson's last name for all of us. We were taking a huge risk. If we'd somehow given ourselves away, we'd walk right into the hands of the police. If we hadn't, we had no plan. Only one thing was certain: The little money we had wouldn't last long.

"Get out the maps." Mom's voice snapped us to action. She suddenly looked very serious. In the days since we'd left Kansas, she had remained upbeat and excited. Now a wave of responsibility seemed to capsize her.

Seated near one of the ferry's huge windows, we spread various maps across a large table. We studied unfamiliar highway numbers and read the names of small towns printed next to tiny dots. As we did, whitecaps formed on the water outside and I began to daydream.

Mom and Jefferson were so engrossed in their maps that they didn't even notice the stranger approaching our table. He was tall and wore a plaid sport coat, dress slacks, and a felt hat with a feather on one side.

"Where are you folks headed?" he asked, startling Mom.

Her reply sounded on edge. "We're not sure."

"I couldn't help overhear your conversation," the stranger said. "It sounds like you're looking for a new place to live."

We should have asked his name or what he wanted. We were certainly the oddest-looking family aboard the ship. Mom was carrying Trixie in an oversized purse, I refused to let go of my half-deflated basketball, and Jefferson was the only black man on board. When I considered how we looked, I began to realize most people actually seemed to be avoiding us. If any of us wondered why the stranger had approached, we never had time to ask.

"You might try Sequim," he said. "They'll accept you there. People from all over the world are relocating there."

Then he touched the brim of his feathered hat and walked away. We re-entered the US in Port Angeles, Washington, a small timber and fishing town on the northern edge of the Olympic Peninsula. Seattle was the nearest big city, three hours away. We passed through customs and immigration without incident and took a taxi, after a few disconcerting looks from the driver, to a nearby hotel. It overlooked a small strip of downtown businesses and a large harbor. A vacancy sign hung outside. In the lobby, the front-desk attendant looked at us and said they were full. Jefferson smiled, said thank you, and ushered us back outside. We walked silently past the vacancy sign. A hotel on the next block also advertised rooms. We opened the front door and went inside. This time, the attendant checked us in.

Later that evening we walked into the downtown area. Standing on the waterfront, we looked back toward Canada. A huge oil tanker moved silently along the Strait of Juan de Fuca, the same body of water we'd crossed earlier that day. On the other side, I could see the lights of Victoria, British Columbia. The smell of saltwater hung in the air.

The next morning we found a car dealership. Jefferson eyed a turquoise Studebaker sedan on the lot. He drove it around the block. When he returned, he took four hundred dollars from his wallet and bought the car. Our bags fit easily in the trunk. I sat in back, Mom carried Trixie in the passenger seat, and Jefferson drove.

Blue Mountain Road leaves US Highway 101 about midway between Port Angeles and Sequim, towns separated by fifteen miles of a one-lane highway. It was one of the more rural roads in an already rural part of western Washington. Shortly after leaving the highway, the road climbs steeply into the foothills of the Olympic Mountains. Large farms and old barns bracket the narrow road.

As Jefferson drove us up Blue Mountain for the first time, the Studebaker began to groan. The possibility of breaking down suddenly seemed very real. I thought, *what if the police show up to help? Will they find out who we were and send us back to Kansas? Are they following us already?*

As the Studebaker pushed forward, I considered the terrible consequences of failure. I distracted myself by spotting deer in nearby meadows as we passed. In some ways, the landscape wasn't so different from the outskirts of Edwardsville. In others, it was half a world away. At their far edges, the fields grew into thick forests. As we kept climbing, I began to feel certain about one thing: No one would find us up here.

It took half an hour to reach our destination. Earlier that morning, Jefferson had seen a job listed in a local newspaper for a ranch caretaker. When he called, the owner said to stop by.

As we neared the top of Blue Mountain Road, I saw a large house surrounded by broad meadows and dense stands of Douglas fir trees with white pole fences, marking the vast boundaries of the ranch. Dozens of deer grazed in the distance. Mr. Chapel, the man who had placed the caretaker ad, was expecting us. Jefferson turned up the driveway and parked. A barn and a small trailer stood nearby. As we opened the car doors, two dogs greeted us. Behind them, a tall rancher with wide shoulders, a large frame, and graying hair walked toward us from the house. A silver belt buckle from his waist shone in the sun, and he carried a cowboy hat in his left hand.

"You must be Jefferson," he said.

"Yes, sir. And you must be Mr. Chapel." Jefferson motioned toward Mom and me. "This is my wife, Sydney, and my number one son, Scottie."

Mr. Chapel took a long look at us. If he was surprised Jefferson was black and Mom wasn't, he didn't show it.

"Nice to meet you folks," he said. He shook our hands and put on his hat. "Well, we better take a look around."

It was a large spread with open fields, trees, fences, ponds, and horses. As he showed us around, Mr. Chapel asked Jefferson about his experience with animals and land. He must have been satisfied with Jefferson's answers because he soon showed us the caretaker's residence. It was a trailer, smaller than our trailer back home, but at least there were two bedrooms.

"That's about all there is," Mr. Chapel said. "If you want, you can stay for a few days and see how you like the place."

Jefferson's smile was as big as I'd seen since before we left Kansas.

For the next few days, Mr. Chapel showed us how he liked things done. He kept his ranch in good working order and expected the same from us. The work wasn't hard. Jefferson mowed the meadows to just the right level for the deer, put out salt licks, and kept oats in the troughs for the horses. Mom fed the dogs and looked after the big house when Mr. Chapel was away. I fed the fish in two ponds. For that, Mr. Chapel paid us room and board.

Admittedly, my job was the easiest. Sometimes, tossing food into the ponds, I thought about the day Mom, Jefferson, and I went fishing outside Edwardsville. It was one of the happiest days I could remember. As I daydreamed atop Blue Mountain Road, I thought about Dad.

I can't tell people much about him. He never, or almost never, touched or abused me directly. But it was the fear of his temper escalating out of control—the sense that anything could displease him at any time—that kept me on guard as a child. He was large, even obese. I never wanted to look like him. It didn't help when so many people said "you look just like your father." He was a man of the cloth, but we never prayed or sang or had joy at home. There were a few okay memories in spite of his terrible abuse of my mother. Those days before school, he would make me breakfast after my mom had left to teach school; these were tolerable times if I didn't spill anything or question how the eggs were cooked or ask too many questions.

There were the rare occasions when he would wrestle or, better yet, play basketball with me. Most of the time, I played basketball by myself, pretending to be both teams. As an only child, I learned how to use my imagination for almost everything. What I didn't understand so outweighed what I did. I never understood why he hit my mom. I never understood why he kept a diary about how crazy Mom was, and I never understood why a local hairdresser from church was always at our house with her husband and son. My parents rarely socialized with anyone because my dad was so mean, but they were the one family from church he always wanted to hang out with, and my mom began to notice that her hairdresser was often at the parsonage. She was supposed to be Mom's best friend.

A few weeks after we started at Mr. Chapel's, Mom and Jefferson began looking for more work. We had a roof over our heads, but we still needed a way to make actual money. They took me with them to the local farm labor office, little more than a trailer near the highway. A woman inside sat at a table. She was smoking a cigarette and thumbing through a box of well-worn index cards.

"How can I help you folks?" she asked. "You look new."

"Yes ma'am, we are *brand* new," Jefferson replied. "They said you might be able to help us find work."

"Well, now," the woman replied, pausing to take a drag of her cigarette. "Let me see what I can do."

As she flipped through her cards, she chatted lightly with Jefferson. She had only one leg. She said her name was Marge.

"Can you do farm work?" she asked.

"Girl!" Jefferson exclaimed. "I've done farm work my whole life. I was raised on a farm."

"Well, it's still early for raspberries. You and your wife could do that, even the boy. There's also hay. She snuffed out her smoke and looked across the table.

"Why don't you head over to Cameron Farm? They've got some early strawberries. The work ain't easy, but it pays."

The day we spent in the strawberry fields still stands as one of the hardest of my life. Everyone but us was an immigrant farm worker. Take it from me, there's no harder job than picking strawberries. If you sit down, you can't move along the rows. If you stand, you can't reach the fruit. The only way to pick strawberries with any success is to squat. When pain engulfs your body, you know you're in the right position.

In the fields, small groups spread out and picked as much fruit as they could as fast as they could. Payment depended on how much you harvested. Years after our day among the strawberry rows, Mom still liked to remind me how I whined the entire time. As I recall, so did she. Of the three of us, the only one who was any good at picking strawberries was Jefferson, and he didn't complain once. In fact, I think he might have been whistling or singing.

Mom enrolled me in Sequim Middle School. Less than two months remained before summer. I avoided other kids as much as possible because we feared being discovered. As the weeks passed, I noticed how late the sun stayed out. By June, I could see across the ranch until past ten o'clock.

We continued to make a home for ourselves at Mr. Chapel's place. Jefferson built a coffee table from a sheet of plywood and two tree trunks. Mom finished it with dark stain and hummingbird decals. With the start of summer, we also began exploring the mountains above us. We'd leave straight from the caretaker's residence and hike until the sky turned pink. Our best walks took us to viewpoints overlooking the Strait of Juan de Fuca and Vancouver Island.

We drove down Blue Mountain Road almost every day. At the bottom we stopped at a small grocery store beside the highway. On the way, we often saw a group of kids playing outside an old farmhouse. One day a woman who lived next door to the farmhouse waved us down. Jefferson pulled over, and mom rolled down the window.

"I hear you're staying at the Chapel ranch," the woman said. She introduced herself and her kids, and she invited Mom and Jefferson in for coffee. Our families became quick friends. When they asked us to their church, Jefferson was elated. The first time we went, his voice dominated the sanctuary. We began to attend regularly and made more friends. When people asked where we were from, we told them Missouri. None of us felt good about lying.

One Sunday they asked Jefferson to preach. Jefferson almost always sang a song at the end of his sermon, especially when he was filled with the Holy Spirit. I remember the song he sang that day, one of my favorites. "I . . . Love the Lord, I love the Lord. I . . . Love the Lord, he brought me out and saved me from my sins. I love the Lord." No one in this all-white congregation, located in the farthest northwest corner of the United States you could possibly be in, had ever heard anything like it. Immediately after, you could hear only silence, and then Jefferson received lots of "amens" and everyone seemed happy to have him there.

But a short time later, the full-time pastor explained to us that because Jefferson was black and not properly ordained in this church denomination, he couldn't preach anymore. The reality was that with our family makeup, we couldn't escape racism anywhere in the United States. While it was more nuanced in Sequim than it was in Kansas, it was still here nonetheless.

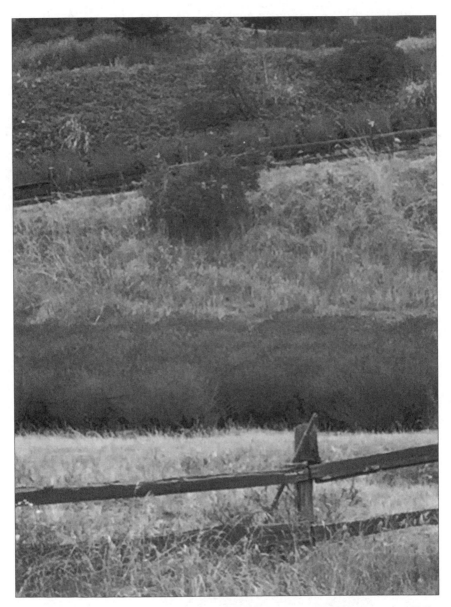

Lavender fields in Sequim's Dungeness Valley

Mom called Grandpa weekly. He said Dad hadn't stopped looking for us and that he had been given legal custody of me. It was strange to think about. In some ways, Dad already seemed like a distant memory. In other ways, he lurked around every corner waiting to pounce.

───────

Jefferson continued to visit Marge at the farm labor extension office. When a full-time position opened at Graysmarsh Farm, she told him about it. Soon afterward, we left Blue Mountain. Mr. Chapel was sorry to see us go, but he knew we couldn't turn down the opportunity. The new job came with a house *and* a paycheck. We thanked Mr. Chapel for everything he'd done. I doubt he ever realized how crucial he was to our family's survival.

Graysmarsh Farm was a registered Guernsey dairy and one of the largest berry-picking operations in the country. It was also home to abundant wildlife. Jefferson milked cows and did odd jobs around the farm. Along with steady pay and half a duplex on the main Graysmarsh property, we also received all the free milk we could drink.

Around this time, I started seventh grade. I also began to think less about Kansas. I still wasn't supposed to tell anyone where we'd come from, but it didn't seem to matter. We'd made it. Dad had no idea where we were.

Jefferson worked long hours on the farm, I went to school, and Mom managed the house. She worked hard to make the duplex feel like home. She painted and put up bright wallpaper, and she upholstered an old couch in red velvet. We didn't have much money, but we didn't need a lot either. We were close to the beach, and the three of us often went there on weekends to walk Trixie and drag driftwood from the surf. We had a roof over our heads. More important, we were free from violence. I was even making friends at school.

In Sequim, our family was different from everyone else and that made us special. People still stared, but we couldn't fault them for it. Many had never seen a black man before, let alone a mixed-race couple. People were understandably curious. Most were also kind. In November of 1970, as we sat down to our first Thanksgiving in Sequim, we had plenty of reasons to express gratitude. Gone were fear and abuse. We had escaped Dad and Kansas and racial violence—and everything else that once had held us back. Together, we had begun a new life. In the course of seven months, our futures had changed. As Jefferson said grace before dinner, I finally felt safe.

Ending Prejudice Based on the Color of Our Skin

"I have a dream that all God's children will be seen as equal regardless of the color of their skin."

—Martin Luther King Jr.

Since I moved back to Washington, DC, to take my position with Global Impact, I have been compelled to visit the Martin Luther King Jr. Monument frequently. MLK Day is an official holiday for Global Impact. The MLK Jr. stamp sits on my desk as a paper weight embedded in a piece of white marble, not unlike the monument itself. The stamp was a gift from Sydney, my mom, when she was the Supervisor of the Sequim post office, one of the many jobs she held as the bread winner of our family.

On the day Martin Luther King Jr. was killed, Sydney led the charge to insist that all students, not just the black students she taught in her class, be allowed to leave early. She believed that if all students, black and white, were dismissed from school at the same time, then no one group or the other would feel they were being singled out in an effort to curb the violence that we faced around the country as a result of Martin Luther King Jr.'s assassination.

Since I grew up during a time when prejudice was rampant, and the small town where we lived did not accept the interracial marriage between my mom and Jefferson Jackson, we were often ostracized. Because of the color of Jefferson's skin, the Sequim families didn't want their daughters to date me. Skin color has so often played a role in the inequality in our society and throughout the world.

On January 18, 2016, in recognition of MLK Jr. Day (not in celebration), twenty thousand people came together in the FEDEX field where the "Red Skins" play—a name that is accepted by too many. They were there to protest the violence against people of color in the United States. Black Lives Matter took over and blocked the San Francisco Bay Bridge.

Immigration reform for men, women, and children from Central and Latin America can't get through Congress, partly because of our prejudice. Wikipedia lists 120 pages of atrocities against people of color over the past century. We elected a black president only to find that many people treated him and his family without due respect for eight years, largely because of our prejudice.

I wasn't as active in the Obama Campaign for President as I had been in the Clinton presidential campaigns, but I had the privilege to take Sydney and my daughter Lindsay to the 2008 Inauguration in Washington, DC. We stood underneath the Capitol and the inaugural podium. It was bitterly cold, but we listened proudly as the first African American president of the United States of America was sworn into office with his family looking on—we knew the world had changed and each of us had played a part. Four years later, I would take Lindsay, the twins, John Oppenheimer, and his daughter Jeni, who was working with me at Global Impact, to the second term inauguration of President Barak Obama, perhaps just as unprecedented.

I didn't know what my life would be like when I pleaded to my mother, "Take me with you." But I am so glad she did and that Jefferson Jackson was there to join us and change our lives forever, as part of our own extraordinary journey and our own contribution as an interracial family to defeat the history of prejudice in America.

African Americans constitute nearly 1 million of the total 2.3 million incarcerated population in the United States. The mass incarceration of black men is illustrated by the fact that there are more African American men incarcerated in the US than the total prison population in India, Argentina, Canada, Lebanon, Japan, Germany, Finland, Israel, and England combined. In 2013, 745,000 African-American men were behind bars. From Ferguson, Missouri, to Baltimore, Maryland, police brutality against African American men and communities is significant. A black man is killed every 28 hours by police or vigilantes. It is unfortunate, but the color of our skin still matters in America.

It's critical in this country—and in the world—that we take racial discrimination seriously. People of color and other ethnicities continue to be discriminated against. We must advocate for change both here in the United States and in other countries where people are at risk. The Global Goals and the focus on eliminating inequality represents an opportunity for humanity to fulfill Martin Luther King Jr.'s dream that someday we no longer see the color of a person's skin but rather we see that person for who they are. There is still far too much racial inequality in this world, and we have the power to work toward a better, more inclusive society.

10 REDUCED INEQUALITIES

GLOBAL GOAL 10

Reduced Inequalities

Reduce inequality within and among countries

Photo by Jonathan Torgovnik for AJWS

In Liberia, members of the Jogbahn clan saved their village from an attempted land grab, with help from AJWS grantee Sustainable Development Institute (SDI). SDI helped eleven towns in Grand Bassa County push back on a British-owned palm oil company attempting to grab their land to extend their plantation. The fight took years, but the villagers eventually prevailed. AJWS continues to support SDI to promote justice and ensure the rights of local people are protected and respected.

Charities in Action

American Jewish World Service (AJWS) works to realize human rights and end poverty in the developing world. AJWS promotes civil and political rights; advances sexual health and rights; defends access to food, land and water; and aids communities in the aftermath of disasters.

The Global Justice Center (GJC) works for peace, justice, and security by enforcing international laws that protect human rights and promote gender equality.

CHAPTER FOUR

Don't Forget Me

November 30, 1970, dawned cold. It was the Monday after Thanksgiving. At school most of the kids stayed inside. Back in Kansas, we would have considered the same day warm for late November. In Edwardsville Mom and I had often played outside after a winter storm, when thick blankets of snow smothered the landscape. One time, Dad joined us and we tossed snowballs playfully and fell to the ground to make snow angels with our bundled bodies. I was excited when Dad came out to play. During every moment of fun, I hoped it was the beginning of more moments; I wished it would last.

It seems ironic that I would think about Kansas that cold Monday after Thanksgiving. I remember standing at my locker between classes, and I can still feel the tap on my shoulder as I turned to see the principal and a police officer behind me. I froze. I think some small part of me knew this moment would come. As much as I wanted to believe Dad had stopped looking for me, I knew it wasn't true. As long as Mom and I were free and living with Jefferson, he wouldn't rest. For him, giving up would mean losing. More than that, it would mean perceived social shame wherever he went. He needed control. It was important that he not feel embarrassed at all costs, and we were embarrassments.

When I first reentered the school system, Mom had walked into the administrative office and enrolled me as Scott Jackson, my new identity. But later in the day after she had left, the office summoned

me to obtain more details for ordering my records from my prior
school. When they asked me what name my records would be under,
I gave them my real name. So either my former school called the
police or the police were tracking the school right from the beginning.

That Monday after Thanksgiving, walking from my locker
toward the principal's office, I felt as if Dad were dragging me by
the ear. Every kid in the hall stared. A few minutes later, looking out
the back of a patrol car, I saw my classmates press their faces against
classroom windows and watch me disappear. An hour later, I entered
a juvenile detention center on the far outskirts of Port Angeles. During
the drive, two plain-clothed officials bracketed me in the backseat.
They told me Mom was being notified of my whereabouts and that
she was facing contempt of court charges and likely would face kidnapping charges. They also said I'd be sent back to Kansas.

Built of cement and ash-colored stucco, the detention center
looked like a fortress. In the lobby, a guard emptied my pockets and
led me further into the building to a small room with a single bed.
It was late afternoon by the time Mom and Jefferson arrived. Mom's
eyes were red, and Jefferson looked disheartened.

"I'm so sorry," Mom said through tears. "I don't know what we
could have done . . ."

Her voice trailed off. Jefferson held her hand as she struggled to
find her words. She was still crying when I asked how they found out
I'd been taken. A police officer had knocked on the door of the duplex
and told her, and she had run barefoot to find Jefferson. They drove
as fast as they could to meet me but were forced to wait. That's when
they found a lawyer.

They didn't get a chance to tell me much more. The guard only
allowed us a few minutes before interrupting. As Mom and Jefferson
left, I walked back to my new room. That night I ate dinner in the
cafeteria with a boy from a nearby Indian reservation. I remember
thinking he was bigger than me. He had dark skin and a long black
braid that hung down his back. He grew up on the coast, but his

parents had died. His foster parents hit him, so he ran away. When he got caught stealing he ended up in the detention center.

Two days after I was taken from school, Mom and Jefferson entered a courtroom in Port Angeles. Across the aisle, Dad sat in silence. In the hall a police officer stood next to me as I strained to hear the judge. Attorney Brooke Taylor argued our case. Mom and Jefferson had found him in a small office above a bank in downtown Port Angeles, and he quickly accepted them as clients. Taylor was twenty-seven years old and less than two years out of law school. He had recently been elected county prosecuting attorney but had yet to take office. Our case struck a chord with the young lawyer.

Taylor had had only a few hours to prepare since meeting Mom and Jefferson. From outside the courtroom, I could hear him argue that the Kansas order giving Dad custody was racist and that the court had no legal reason to take me from Mom. I also heard him tell the judge about Dad's abuse.

That night in the detention center, I stared at the ceiling of my room and let the tears stream down my face. The next morning, Taylor filed a motion to stay the proceedings pending an appeal. He argued that by upholding the Kansas order, the court would strip Mom of all parental rights. The judge didn't budge. As his gavel crashed, Dad finally won.

Dad left the courtroom first.

"Scottie," he said, stopping in the hall. "I know this must be hard for you. . . ."

I began to feel ill. His mouth was still moving, but I couldn't hear him. My head began to spin, my stomach burned, and I wanted to scream. My throat was too dry to speak. I thought I might collapse, and I stared at the floor to steady myself. When I looked up again, I saw his back as the outside door closed behind him.

Mom and Jefferson appeared next. Tears poured from Mom's eyes. She could barely speak. "I'm so sorry. We tried."

Jefferson put his hand on my shoulder.

"It's not over, Boy. We'll keep fighting." His grip felt strong. I believed him.

Mom composed herself. Then they told me an appeal was still possible. Brooke Taylor said he would continue working on our case. A higher court might reconsider the Kansas ruling, something this judge refused to do. For now, I had to return to Kansas.

On Sunday morning, Mom and Jefferson came for their final visit at the detention center.

"We'll keep fighting," mom said. "And I'll write to you every day."

I believed her. As we spoke, a guard stood outside the visitors' room. Mom grabbed my hand and squeezed hard. "People are praying for you," she said.

Then she began to whisper. "We have something for you. Something you need to keep close." She reached into her purse and handed me a Bible. She flipped it open, and I saw the names and phone numbers of old friends and contacts from Kansas and across the country written in light pencil. She turned to Psalm 23. Grandma and Grandpa Hughes' phone number appeared in the margin.

"Just in case," Mom said.

I didn't understand what she meant. Before I could ask, she handed me a dark green knit hat. "A woman in the church made this special hat for you," she said.

It looked warm. But there was something else. Leaning over, Mom gently pulled back some of the stitching. Between layers of yarn I saw money sewn inside. When she let go, the double stitching and green yarn made it invisible again.

Suddenly I was crying.

"What do you want me to do?" I asked.

"You need to do what's right," Mom said softly. "No matter what, we'll be here."

Then our time was up. The guard entered to take me back to my room. I hugged Mom and Jefferson with all the strength I had. I didn't want to let go. I never wanted to let go.

"We love you," Jefferson said through tears.

"I love you, too," I said. "Don't forget me."

On Monday morning a woman brought a folded pile of clothes to my room at the detention center. I dressed slowly. When I arrived in the lobby, Dad stood up.

"Hi, Scottie." That was all he could say before I exploded.

"Go to hell, you bastard. You don't want me."

I wanted to punch him in the face. I wanted to take every bit of anger I had and throw it at him. What could he do? We were still inside the detention center. He wouldn't dare hit me in front of witnesses. But who was I kidding? He weighed a hundred pounds more than me— by this time, my dad had become obese. Even if he didn't hit me here, he'd certainly make me pay later. *Not now*, I told myself. *Not like this.*

The drive to Kansas passed slowly. For much of the trip I refused to speak. Every time we stopped, I looked for ways to run away. When we pulled off the interstate for food and gas, Dad followed me to the bathroom. Every hour in the car seemed like another eternity away from Sequim. Four days after leaving Port Angeles, Dad pulled up the gravel drive in front of Tall Oaks. As he did, a crash of memories collapsed around me. Everything looked exactly the same.

I returned to school in Linwood. I'd been gone less than a year. Rather than nostalgia, I felt apathy. Dad picked me up each afternoon. I wasn't allowed to ride the bus. If Dad couldn't make it on time, he sent Slim, the camp handyman. I couldn't leave the house alone. The one thing I could do was play basketball in the yard.

A few weeks after we got back, Dad said, "I think you need to see a counselor. You've been through a lot."

"I don't need a counselor," I argued. "I just need my mother."

"Well, we're going to see this counselor; the courts are requiring it, and it will be good for you."

"Don't make me see a counselor—you'll regret it," I threatened.

We took the elevator up a few floors and walked into the waiting room. Chairs with green cushions were lined up against the wall, in front of which stood a table with a selection of magazines. A woman came out to greet us and asked me to come in while Dad remained in the waiting room. She had brunette hair, glasses, a medium build, and a round face. She looked safe enough initially, but when she began to speak, I knew I couldn't trust her.

She said, "So I understand you may be having a hard time now that you're back with your real dad. That's natural, especially with the additional complications of being with your mom and a black man. I'm here to help you talk about that." She went on about how she felt bad for me that I had to spend time with Mom and Jefferson and felt it was important to make adjustments, talk about it, and reenter the white world. "It must have been tough living with a black man," she sympathized.

Jefferson and Sydney Lou

"Listen, you bitch, there was nothing hard about living with Jefferson and my mom," I spewed. "That man out there beat my mom. You can send me back to the fucking judge and I'm going to tell him what you said and how prejudiced you are and that my dad is a wife beater, and I don't need any goddamned counseling from you."

Then I picked up a side table and threw it across the room. She walked out to the waiting room and finally came back, and then we left.

Dad said, "You'll never have to see another counselor again." We never went back.

I saw Grandma and Grandpa a few weeks after my return to Kansas. They came to Tall Oaks with Ricky and Patty early one afternoon just before Christmas. Grandma had baked a cake, and they brought me some pictures of Mom and Jefferson taken in Sequim after I left. They brought me a small artificial Christmas tree with handmade baked ornaments of all of them, reminding me of our life in Sequim. Dad inspected everything before I could have it. That evening, as I walked the four of them to their car, Grandpa asked if I had received any of Mom's letters. I hadn't.

"Listen," I said, "you have to get me out of here."

"We will, Scottie, but we don't know much more about the courts and the appeal your mom is trying to make, but she's trying. So don't lose hope."

"Well, I won't, but isn't there anything else we can do? Because he has a gun underneath his bed and I don't want to be here."

"What kind of gun?" Grandpa Whitey asked.

"A handgun," I replied.

"Has he brought it out to you? Has he hit you?"

"No, not really, but I don't feel comfortable here."

Shortly after they left, the police showed up at the office door and Dad answered. They told him they'd received a complaint that he had a gun and his son was scared for his life, and they came in and questioned us. My father was livid.

As winter settled over Kansas and Tall Oaks, I felt the cold sting of distance between Mom, Jefferson, and me. With it came the realization that I wasn't thinking about them as much. Instead, I was starting to adjust to life with Dad. I started to doubt how much they could do. Nearly two months had passed and I still hadn't received a single letter. I didn't think they had given up—I knew something was wrong because my grandfather had told me my mom had been writing to me—but with each week, the memories started to fade. And I was guarded all the time. My dad rarely left me alone. I knew it was pretty hopeless and didn't think Mom and Jefferson could get a court appeal. Who was going to listen to a white woman and a black man? My memories would fade, and my reality became the reality of living there. I was afraid I was going to forget my mom.

Kansas was home now, after all.

Finding the Forgotten Children of the World

My three daughters mean the world to me. I have lived and I will die believing they are the most precious gift I have ever been given. I have worked hard to make sure they never have to experience what I did as a child. Lindsay, the oldest, and her identical twin sisters, Haley and Allison, are all three like stars in the sky for me. We are forever thankful that they grew up with all the love and care we could give them.

Unfortunately, millions of children throughout the world still need our help. There are children who are neglected, kids in less than ideal foster-care situations, and young adults on the run. There are also children in third-world countries who are malnourished, dying of preventable diseases, and at risk for being abducted and raped or forced into armies as child soldiers.

The number of children from broken homes has more than tripled since 1950. Neglect and abuse of children in the United States has also more than tripled, with a 134 percent increase since 1980. More than 250,000 children age out of foster care each year, leaving more than half a million children remaining in foster care each year in the United States.

Thirty percent of all young people under the age of 18 live below the poverty line with three out of every seven now living in poverty. It is estimated that more than fourteen million children live in poverty in the United States. That number is even higher throughout the world. One in three African American children live in unsecure households. As many as 18,000 children in the world under five years of age will die of preventable diseases, such as pneumonia and diarrhea, each day. More than six million children will die every year from such causes.

Globally, half of the deaths of children under five result from malnutrition. Four out of every ten children fail to meet even basic dietary standards. Between the year 2000 and the present day, ten million children under eighteen have lost one or more of their parents to HIV AIDS, and malaria takes the lives of four out of five of all children infected.

While these numbers may seem staggering and overwhelming, there is so much that each of us can do to make the world better for children. We can give our time, and we can donate to the programs that are implementing real concrete solutions in some of the areas that need them most.

We cannot forget our children—they are our future.

GLOBAL GOAL 11

Sustainable Cities and Communities

Make cities and human settlements inclusive, safe, resilient and sustainable

©2014 Jon Warren/World Vision

Bangladesh is one of the world's most densely populated countries—and one of the most dangerous for a child. All day, every day, children are trafficked across the border. They are sold to brothels. They have little hope of escape. Sonali and her sister live at the Hat Khola brothel with their mother. Sonali's mother, Reshma, was trafficked at age 10. "Daughters in the brothel learn about the sex trade," says Reshma. "I don't want that."*

—WORLD VISION

From "A Safe Place for Children Living in a Brothel"

Names have been changed to protect identities.

Charities in Action

UNITED STATES FUND

UNICEF strengthens child protection systems and promotes positive social norms in all contexts (development and emergency) to prevent and respond to violence, exploitation, and abuse directed at children.

Save the Children believes every child deserves a future. In the U.S. and around the world, we ensure children have the opportunity to learn and develop the skills they need to succeed. We do whatever it takes for children—every day and in times of crisis—transforming their lives and the future we share.

World Vision®

World Vision's programs focus on activities that prevent children from falling into crisis or harmful situations; protect those who are in immediate danger; and restore child survivors of abuse, exploitation, or violence.

CHAPTER FIVE

I Love You

My decision to run away began with a trip to the post office. That afternoon, Dad picked me up from school, parked outside the tiny post office in Linwood, and told me to wait in the car. I could see the service counter through the large outside windows. Because it was snowing, and because I was cold, and maybe because I just wanted to get Dad mad, I waited only a few minutes before going in. By the time Dad noticed, it was too late. He tried to shuffle the envelope to the bottom of his stack, but I'd already seen Mom's handwriting.

"Hey, that's mine," I yelled. "Give me that."

The post office clerk turned toward me and back to Dad. I knew instantly I had committed a mortal sin. I'd embarrassed my father in public. Dad turned his entire body toward me. His face warped, his teeth clenched, and I could see him start to shake.

"Get in the car," he ordered. His voice sounded intense, measured, staccato.

He stepped toward me. I backed away. "Move!" he yelled.

On the ride home, Dad remained silent. I knew not to speak when he got this way. I wouldn't wait long. He had something I wanted, and I'd do anything to get it. Inside the house, I followed him to the kitchen.

In a start, he turned and yelled, "Go to your room. Now!"

He towered over me. He looked exactly like he had so many times before when I'd watched him hit Mom or bang on the bathroom door as she cried inside. I knew he'd hit me if I didn't move. I slumped away and started toward the hall. Just once, I looked back. Dad had set the mail on the counter and started to take off his coat. I lunged for the envelope. When I felt it between my fingers I started to run. Dad charged after me. I darted down the hall and turned into my room. But I was too slow. Dad's weight crashed on top of me. His fury landed with a heavy thud, and my arm slammed against the bedpost. My body shuddered as he pinned me to the floor. His fist smashed against my ribs. Pain tore through me. Dad's immense weight felt as though it might kill me. Just then, Dad grabbed the letter from my hand, got up, and slammed the door.

My head spun like the snow swirling outside. Memories flashed to mind: *Mom and Jefferson walking in the hills above Sequim and sitting in a field at dusk . . . Dad choking Mom and throwing her against a wall . . . The bright light of a single train rushing toward me down the tracks near the old parsonage in Edwardsville.*

I don't recall everything I thought about in those few moments. More than anything, I was scared. Scared of Dad. Scared I'd never see Mom again. Scared of what would happen next.

I was still sitting on the floor when Dad returned to my room. His body filled the doorway.

"Here's your stupid letter." He threw it on my bed and walked away.

On the outside of the envelope, Mom's handwriting looked just as I remembered. I began to imagine all the things she must have written. She would tell me about her and Jefferson, about Sequim, and about our friends from church. I picked up the envelope and reached inside. A single sheet of paper came out. Unfolding it, I saw only three words: *I love you.*

I felt stunned. That was *it?* Didn't she have anything else to say? Did she even care about me anymore? I'd hoped Mom's letter would bring some kind of relief. Instead it only confused me. As I lay in my room, aching, I realized something. In that moment, silent and in pain, staring at the ceiling, I grasped the reality before me. I'd had my suspicions. I suppose that's why I went into the post office to begin with. But now I knew for sure. Ever since I had been back, Dad had been keeping my mail from me. Mom wrote only three words because she knew Dad wouldn't let me read anything else.

I began to move almost as soon as I had the thought. Since my return to Kansas, I'd been careful to keep the Bible and knit cap Mom had given me away from Dad. Now I reached under my bed and pulled the Bible from its hiding spot. Inside my closet, I grabbed a duffel bag and put my basketball inside. It was the same one I ran away with the first time. Mom and Jefferson had left it for me after their final visit to the detention center in Port Angeles. I moved quickly around my room to get some underwear, a sweatshirt, a couple of comic books, and the knit cap stored carefully on the top shelf of my closet. I zipped up the duffel, and then walked to my window and dropped the bag into the snow.

I could jump out the window easily and be okay. But if I did and Dad came looking for me, I wouldn't get far. I closed the window, pulled on my heaviest coat, stuffed the cap into one of my pockets. I headed down the hall where I found Dad in his office.

"Sorry about the letter," I said. "I shouldn't have done that. Anyway, I guess she didn't have much to say."

Dad looked up at me. "I guess not."

"Can I go for a walk? I want to see the snow. I won't go far."

Maybe he felt bad about hitting me, or maybe he just realized he couldn't keep me in my room forever. "Stay close," he said. "It's getting dark."

Stepping outside, I pulled on the knit cap. Cold air bit at my face as I circled back to my bedroom window to retrieve the duffel. I slung it over my shoulder and hurried across the yard. I skirted some nearby trees and made a beeline for the camp mess hall. Fresh snow covered the ground. I left a trail of tennis shoe tracks behind me.

The door to the commons swung open easily. It was empty inside. I walked straight to the payphone. The number was written inside my Bible, but I didn't need to look.

"Scottie, is that you?" Grandpa's voice came from the other end of the line.

"Yes. I'm running away. I want to go home. I want to go back to Sequim." My voice sounded anxious. "It's snowing. I don't know what to do."

"Hold on. Don't go anywhere. I'll be right back." Grandpa set down the phone. Across the mess hall, I heard pots clang. Someone was in the kitchen. Before I could react, Grandpa came back on the line.

"Listen carefully, Scottie. Do you remember the horse ranch in De Soto? We bought Midnight there. It's about five miles from you. Can you get there?"

I remembered the ranch and the day Mom and Grandpa took me there. I didn't know where it was, but I knew how to get to De Soto. It wouldn't be easy in the snow, but I didn't have a choice.

"I can get there," I said. "I'll find the ranch."

"When you do, knock on the door. Tell them Whitey sent you. Say your ride is late because of the snow. A car will come pick you up. You'll hear three honks. That will be your signal to leave."

More sounds from the kitchen.

"Grandpa, I have to go." I was whispering now.

"We love you, Scottie. Be safe. We'll see you soon."

I hung up the phone quietly and turned for the door. I moved quickly back outside. Looking down, I realized my feet were already wet from snow seeping through my tennis shoes.

The main camp road ran through the property about a hundred feet west of the dining hall. I ran straight toward it and kept on running. Beyond the road, the oak forest provided cover. Even without leaves, the trees created a nice hiding place. I didn't know how long Dad would let me stay outside before he came looking. Not long, I thought. I moved beyond the edge of the woods to deeper cover. Looking up, I saw a tangled braid of black branches against a dark gray sky. Soft light was reflected from the falling snow.

Suddenly, I heard a rustling. When I turned, two dark eyes stared straight through me. A second later the deer darted through the trees.

I followed its lead. My heart raced. I told myself to keep going until I reached the swimming pool, about a hundred yards up the road.

A chain-link fence surrounded the pool. Beyond it, a hill sloped downward away from the road. I stopped to listen. Quiet. I began to run again, this time toward the open-air chapel farther down the road. *One step at a time. Point to point. Keep moving.*

At the chapel, I again stopped to listen. Nothing. I looked up at the swooping limestone wall and the tall cross that hung from one side. I used to sit in the chapel alone and pray. I'd pray that Dad would stop hitting Mom and that everything would get better. Those prayers never came true. At times I questioned why God had put me in this situation, but I never gave up on my faith. Before I left, I said another quick prayer, the kind you think more than say. *Amen.*

Again I began running.

Back in the woods, I moved quickly toward the bluff near the end of the camp road. I ran hard. I began to breathe heavily. I heard something behind me. I stopped and turned my head. A truck was driving up the road. I could hear it struggling in the snow. I knew it could only be Dad or Slim. I turned back for the bluff and moved deeper into the trees.

I reached the top of the hill well ahead of the truck. Looking down the bluff, I knew this was my last chance to turn around, to create some kind of story about why I had come this far. If I went any farther and got caught, there would be no hiding my motive. I feared what Dad might do when he found me. It didn't matter. I already felt free. Even if the feeling didn't last, I wasn't going to give it up willingly. There was a stillness that settled upon me.

The quiet that surrounded me was more than the ensuing darkness, more than the deafening silence of snow falling, and even more than the hissing sound of the wind. I reached up with my arm and felt the knit hat with the twenty dollar bills sewn inside and adjusted it down over my ears to prevent frostbite from the cold.

I stared across the open distance in front of me. A wide snow-covered field ran along the bottom of the bluff. Beyond was the road to

De Soto. From where the field met the road I figured it was about two miles to the Wyandotte Street Bridge. The bridge crossed the Kansas River into De Soto.

The rumble of the truck snapped me to attention. I looked back just once before darting over the edge of the bluff. As the slope steepened, I began to slide. The snow caused me to move uncontrollably. My tennis shoes provided little traction. Thick bushes tore at my coat.

It took less than a minute to reach the field. Somehow I made it without falling. It was almost completely dark now. I looked back up the bluff. The sound of the truck had stopped. Between the road and me stood only untracked snow. I took off as fast as I could through the shallow snow. Midway across the field I collapsed. A sharp pain shot through my left leg. I rolled on the ground wincing. I tore off my shoe. Blood seeped from my heel. My toes froze. A large thorn stuck through my sock. It somehow had found its way down the side of my shoe before lodging in the bottom of my foot. I squinted back toward the bluff. Darkness was my ally. Anyone standing atop the slope would struggle to see me. Anyone driving by on the road would likely miss me in the snow and dusky light.

My foot throbbed. *No time.* I pulled out the thorn, retied my shoe, and again started to move. Cold air stung my lungs. I reached up and pulled my hat down over my ears.

I arrived at the road and crossed straight to the other side. A thin strip of land separated the street from the railroad berm and tracks. Up and over, I disappeared on the other side of the embankment. A narrow band of trees ran along the riverbank. Through it I heard the soft lapping of water against the shore. I was exactly where I wanted to be. The rail berm hid me from the road, and I could follow the tracks toward De Soto. This was my territory, the exact kind of spot where I spent endless hours when back in Edwardsville; I roamed the north shore of the same river, the same tracks.

A faint glow of light hung low in the distant vespertine sky. Catching my breath, I thought about Mom and Jefferson. *What would they think if they knew where I was? Has Grandpa called them? Are they wondering about me right now?* The cold air snapped me back to the present moment.

There was only one way to get to De Soto: the Wyandotte Street Bridge. Almost instinctively, I reached up and touched my hat. Pinching it, I felt the money sewn inside. The snowfall had nearly stopped, and a cold wind blew undiluted down the tracks. I pulled the hat tighter over my ears. My left foot still stung. I didn't know how long it would take for Grandpa's connection, whoever it was, to drive to the horse ranch, but I knew I needed to get there first.

I started jogging east along the edge of the tracks. The snow cover was lighter here than in the field. After a few minutes, the tracks crossed a small stream that ran toward the river. From here, it was about a mile and a half to Wyandotte Street. I kept moving along the bottom of the berm, watching for spikes and other debris in the near darkness. The sound of an engine startled me. It came from the road. I stopped. Whoever it was, they were driving slowly. I lowered my body and climbed the rail berm. In the distance, I saw flashing red and blue police lights. I kept my head to the tracks and watched as the car moved closer.

What are they doing? Are they looking for me? The answers seemed obvious.

I dropped back down to the berm. If someone climbed up the other side, they'd spot me easily. I considered giving up. If I turned myself in, maybe Dad wouldn't be upset. I was colder and colder. I questioned my decision to run away. The thought of trying to find a horse ranch in a town I barely knew began to scare me. *Is it crazy to keep going? Climb over the tracks. You'll be safe. You'll be warm.*

I shook my head in disbelief. What was wrong with me? Dad had just tackled and punched me. Things weren't going to get any better, especially now. I looked toward the faint glow of De Soto. Across the tracks, the flashing lights passed parallel to my position and continued toward Wyandotte Street. As the lights dimmed, I started moving again. The junction of the tracks and Wyandotte Street grew closer with each step. There was only one way to cross the river. *It's a trap.*

It didn't matter. I was out of options. If I couldn't cross the bridge, I couldn't run away. I reached Wyandotte Street about fifteen minutes later. *It's over.*

I looked up at the night sky. Not a single star broke the clouds. I shook my head. *Kansas is home now.*

I climbed the berm slowly to meet my fate. Standing at the junction of the tracks and Wyandotte Street, I looked around. The police lights were gone. Darkness and empty fields surrounded me. To the south, the glow of De Soto appeared brighter across the river.

I began to walk toward the light, keeping a few yards off the street and hugging sparse hedgerows. As I did, I found myself humming a song Jefferson had taught me.

> *We've come this far by faith,*
> *leaning on the Lord;*
> *trusting in His holy word.*
> *He's never failed us yet.*
> *Oh! We can't turn back,*
> *We've come this far by faith.*

I knew I was doing the right thing. Even if I got caught, I had to try to get back to Mom and Jefferson. They'd given up almost everything they had to escape with me the first time. I owed it to them to get back.

Suddenly, headlights appeared behind me. Turning around, I could tell immediately it was a truck. *I'm doomed!*

Part of me wanted to run, but there was no place to go. The only thing on either side of the road was an open field covered in snow. As the truck came closer, I froze. A second later, I realized it wasn't the camp truck. Mixed thoughts raced through my mind. *Lay on the ground. Hide. No. Wait.*

Before I knew it, I was standing in the road waving my arms. The truck stopped. I walked to the passenger-side door. An old man dressed in blue overalls leaned across the bench seat and rolled down the window. I had no idea what to say. I was alone at night in the middle of a storm. He must have thought I was crazy. Maybe I was. Whose idea was it to run away in a storm?

"Can I get a lift to the city limits? I didn't realize how cold it was when I started." My words came without thought. The man looked like he was trying to decide if I was real or some sort of icy hallucination.

"The city limits?" he asked.

"Yeah. I'm meeting a friend."

"Alright. Jump in."

He put the truck in gear and started toward the bridge. The road was slick, and his wheels spun before finding traction. We didn't talk much. I was glad he didn't ask any more questions. It took only a few minutes to cross the bridge and enter De Soto.

"Here you are," he said, pulling over. "You sure I can't take you any farther?"

"No, this is perfect." I opened the door and jumped out. "Thanks."

As he pulled away, I began to walk away from the river. A couple of blocks later, I reached the main road through town. Warm yellow light blazed through the windows of a nearby café. Inside the small restaurant heat surrounded me. A few patrons looked up briefly before returning to their dinner. I quickly saw what I needed. The payphone didn't interest me, but the phonebook did. I flipped through the yellow pages and found the ranch. Spotting the waitress nearby, I asked if she knew how to get there.

"It's not far," she smiled, offering directions. "Keep your eye out. It might be hard to see in the storm."

Outside, the snow was falling more heavily. I pulled my collar up against the cold. It took almost an hour to reach the ranch on the outskirts of town. During that time, not a single car passed on the road. If anyone were to travel this forsaken, snow-covered country road, I would see them but they would not see me.

The ranch looked just as I remembered. A large single-story home, a huge barn, fenced horse rings, and big empty fields now covered in white. I made my way up the driveway to the steps and covered front porch and rang the bell. A man about Grandpa's age opened the door and looked down at me. I recognized his face from the day we bought Midnight. I could tell from his expression he was surprised to see me. I began to rush through my cover story.

The man didn't let me talk long. Maybe he realized how cold I was outside. Standing on his front porch, I began to feel the chill sink in. The walk must have helped keep me warm, because I was suddenly shivering.

Inside, the man asked me to take off my coat and sit down. Then he disappeared to tell his wife they had company. As he did, I took a deep breath. I'd done it. I'd made it from Tall Oaks to the horse ranch without getting caught. It seemed like forever since I'd hung up the phone in the camp mess hall. Now I had a new worry: *Where's my ride?*

When the ranch owner returned, I was standing by a large window looking over the driveway and front yard. His wife stood next to him. She said hello and asked if I wanted cookies and hot chocolate. A few minutes later she found me on the couch, watching TV with her husband. As the minutes ticked by, I grew increasingly anxious. *What if no one comes? How long until these people start to ask questions? Do they know Dad?*

Suddenly, I heard a honk. I looked out the front window and saw headlights in the driveway.

"That's my ride," I said. "Thank you so much."

Stepping off the front porch, I wondered who was in the car. The back door cracked open as I approached. I strained to look inside. Just before I got in I heard the ranch owner's voice behind me: "Tell your Grandpa we said hello."

From inside the car, a deep voice said, "Hurry. Get in."

The driver wasn't alone. Someone else sat in the passenger seat. Glancing over his shoulder, I could see he was holding a shotgun across his lap.

Who are these people? Why should I trust them?

I had little time to think about the answers.

"Lay down. Don't talk. We don't want anyone to know you're back there."

I did what the driver said. As we drove away, I started to pray.

After a few minutes, the driver spoke again.

"Don't worry, Scottie. We're going to get you to your Grandpa."

At least he knows my name.

"If anyone stops us, you're a hitchhiker. We picked you up in the snow. Got it?"

Lying on my back across the seat, I could see the snow falling again. The car moved slowly. I could hear the wiper blades. We were headed toward the Missouri state line. *We're going in the right direction.*

I stayed low and listened as the two men up front started to relax. They spoke in low voices; their tension seemed to be easing.

During the ride, I moved through stages of feeling worried and feeling liberated. Listening to the men talk to each other seemed to help. They were on a mission. On the other hand, thinking about the gun freaked me out. My escape had quickly become more dangerous than I imagined. *What if we're pulled over? Will they shoot a police officer?*

"I'm Jerry, by the way." It was the driver. Looking up, I saw the side of his face in the faint light. "You're doing great back there. Your Grandpa and I go way back. Stay low. The city's coming up."

Nearly an hour elapsed between De Soto and the state line. In good weather the drive would have taken half as long. I never learned the other man's name. As we crossed the border, Jerry said I could sit up as long as I crouched low enough so no one could see me. I began to recognize some of the roads. Crossing the Missouri River, I thought about the last time I visited Grandma and Grandpa's house. It was the night Mom and Jefferson planned our escape—my first escape. The river seemed larger than I recalled. I started to think about some of the times Mom and I drove to Claycomo to get away from Dad. I remembered Mom's bruises, her tears, and how afraid she used to get. Years later I'd learn more about the abuse, about how Mom's friends took her in during those nights she ran from our house, about the bite marks and bruises they saw during those frightening times when they found their friend Sydney at their front door crying and wearing only a nightgown.

"Scottie!" Jerry's voice snapped me back to the moment. "We're here. North Kansas City. I'm going to drop you off at city hall. Don't worry. Your Grandpa's waiting inside."

I was shocked. *City hall? That makes no sense. What are we doing here?*

"What?" I asked.

Jerry hesitated. "Trust me."

"But it's the middle of the night."

"I know. Just trust me."

"Will I see you again?"

"I hope so."

I didn't know much about North Kansas City. Mom went to high school nearby. Grandpa surely knew people here. Beyond that, I only knew it was across the river from Kansas City.

Jerry stopped the car. I grabbed my bag and got out reluctantly.

City hall was a short nondescript building with a large parking lot. Following Jerry's instructions, I walked toward the front door. I didn't feel good about this plan at all. The snow had stopped, and an eerie quiet floated through the air. As I approached the building, Grandpa opened the front door and walked outside. He wore a dark suit and looked serious. Behind him I saw Grandma and Ricky. I could hardly believe it. They rushed past Grandpa. Somewhere between the parking lot and the front doors we collided in a group hug.

Grandpa brought us to attention.

"Listen. We're going inside to talk to a friend. He's a lawyer. Don't worry."

Grandpa's command of the situation relieved me. Standing in front of city hall seemed like the worst possible place to be. But Grandpa Whitey knew what he was doing. Anyway, it seemed that way. At that moment, that was good enough.

We moved quickly inside, down the halls. Turning into one of the offices, I saw a man sitting alone behind a huge desk. Like Grandpa, he wore a dark suit. He began to speak quickly. At first, he recapped what I already knew: Dad had full custody of me; Mom and Jefferson were lucky to avoid kidnapping charges; the Kansas court didn't want anything else to do with our case.

What he said next hit me like an important newsflash: "Your mom won an appeal in Washington. I have no idea how she pulled it off. She must have one hell of an attorney. There's just one problem. The decision has no effect here. Unless you get back to Washington, your dad still has legal custody."

A train could have driven straight through that office and I would have been less shocked. *Mom won! She and Jefferson did exactly what they said they would. They kept fighting for me.*

The attorney turned to Grandpa and offered a smile. "Whitey, you're playing with fire here. There's a warrant pending to search your house. The fact is no court in Kansas or Missouri will side with an unknown judge out West. Not on this."

I felt a new wave of anxiety. If I got caught now, I would find myself right back at Tall Oaks. Only now it would be worse. Dad would lock me down completely. The thought was unbearable.

Grandpa thanked his friend, and we left as quickly as we had arrived. Back outside, Grandpa steered his Cadillac away from city hall. I kept my head low in the backseat. As we drove toward Claycomo, Grandpa hatched a plan.

"You can't come home with us tonight, Scottie," he said. "We're going to drop you at Bill's place. You can stay with him and Dixie. You'll be safe there. Tomorrow you're going back to Sequim."

I'd met Bill Edwards many times around Grandpa's store, but had never been to his house. I didn't know Dixie, his wife, at all. It didn't matter. Driving through the outskirts of Kansas City with Grandma and Grandpa, I started to get the feeling everything would work out.

The police car changed those feelings instantly. Grandpa had taken the main road through Claycomo and driven right past the farm. Across the property, a police cruiser was parked in the drive-way. Grandma spotted it first.

"Scottie! Get on the floor!"

Grandpa's decision to drive that close to the house seemed crazy, which Grandma made sure to tell him. I stayed glued to the backseat for the rest of the ride. Grandpa looked repeatedly in his mirrors to see if we were being followed. When the car stopped, I sat up and looked out the window.

Bill Edwards and my mom had gone to school together. In high school, Bill worked at Grandpa's store. Grandpa took him in as a sort of protégé. Bill later opened his own business and bought property around Claycomo, growing into one of the area's wealthier residents.

"It all started at Hughes Furniture," Grandpa had said more than once.

He turned to look at me in the backseat. "We love you, Scottie. You did great tonight. Now go on. They know you're coming."

No long goodbye. Just a smile and a wave. Too much still on the line. Grandma was still upset about Whitey's risk driving by the farm.

Bill and Dixie answered the front door together. I saw my grand-parents and Ricky drive away as it closed. I didn't know when I would see them again. But I didn't have time to think about it. Bill showed me around the house, and Dixie asked if I wanted any hot chocolate. If nothing else, running away had paid dividends in hot chocolate.

"We're glad you're here," Bill said. "You did the right thing. Your mom is going to be thrilled to see you."

Grandpa trusted Bill more than anyone. He was the only person outside our family who knew where Grandpa stashed his cash around the store and farm. Now he was being trusted with something even more important.

"How do you feel about sleeping in the attic?" Bill asked. "There's a bed up there, and it's a good place to hide. Just in case."

The truth was that nowhere would be completely safe until I got back to Sequim. Even then, there was no telling which court decision would ultimately win out. Right now, though, nothing sounded as good as a bed. I climbed into the attic and fell asleep. Not even Dixie's hot chocolate could wake me.

The sun hadn't yet come up when I awoke. I heard Bill's voice downstairs.

"Time to move, Scottie. Jerry is coming to get you. Dixie is making breakfast."

A few minutes later, still exhausted, I was dressed and watching television. The morning news jolted me. They were talking about me. They gave my name—my real name—my age, and said I was missing. My face flashed across the TV screen.

"Bill! Dixie! I'm on the news. They think I've been kidnapped."

"We have to get you out of here," Bill said, sounding worried. "The sooner you're back with your mom the better."

I scarfed down Dixie's breakfast as fast as I could. Before I finished, I heard Jerry pull up outside.

"Time to go," Bill said. "Jerry will explain everything."

Outside, Jerry motioned to the backseat. This time he was alone. From what I could see, the shotgun was also missing.

"Morning, Scottie." Jerry sounded positively chipper. "Just you and me, kiddo. But I need you to stay down back there."

"Sounds good," I said. "Did you see me on the news?"

"Don't you worry about that. We're getting you out of here."

As we pulled away, Jerry explained the plan.

The drive to Omaha, Nebraska, took four hours. We stopped once to use the restroom. Back in the car, Jerry handed me a white envelope.

"At the airport, I'll go in and pick up your ticket. If anything happens after I leave, do your best to get outside and find me. If you have any problems, use that money. Otherwise give it to your mom."

I opened the envelope. Inside, I saw hundreds of dollars in cash.

"Everything will be okay," Jerry said.

At the airport I waited in a parking lot while Jerry picked up the ticket.

When he returned, he smiled. "You're almost there, Scottie. It's been fun. All you have to do is board the plane. Your mom will be waiting in Seattle."

I couldn't believe it. Less than twenty-four hours had passed since I'd run away from Tall Oaks. Somehow, despite everything, I'd made it this far. I thanked Jerry for all his help and got out of the car.

A few minutes later, walking through the airport, I looked for the quietest spot I could find. When I heard my flight number, I took a quick look around and started for the gate.

Taking off, I noticed how clear the sky was and how beautiful the ground appeared beneath the plane. The storm of yesterday had cleared and in its wake lay below a snowy world of white. It looked just like our front yard outside the parsonage so many years earlier when Mom and Dad and I would go outside and make snow angels and laugh and roll on the ground. How distant the memory seemed. How foreign and irreconcilable with the violence and abuse. Moving west through the blank sky, I put the thought behind me.

A few hours later, peering out the same small window, I saw the Seattle skyline. Inside the airport Mom and Jefferson stood at the gate. They grabbed me, and we hugged for a long time. No one wanted to let go. Mom laughed when she reached for my bag and felt the basketball inside. My good luck charm had worked again.

On the drive home, they told me about the court hearings and how they had won their appeal. They said the fight wasn't over. The appeals court had sent the case back to the county judge for reconsideration—the same judge who sent me back to Kansas.

"This time," Mom said, "he'll have to listen to us."

Her words made me think of something else, something that had happened a few days earlier.

"Thanks for the letter," I said. "I love you, too."

Protecting the Runaway Children

The invisible children of Gulu, sometimes referred to as the night-walkers, are forced to leave their homes and villages each night to find safety in the camps until morning, when they return and attempt to attend school. For more than twenty years, these children and their con-flict have remained unchecked—and invisible to the rest of the world. Like the forgotten children in other parts of the world.

The children of South Sudan and the Democratic Republic of Congo continue to be raped, turned into child soldiers, or forced into servitude. Human trafficking of children for sexual exploitation and forced labor represents an industry with more than $150 billion in annual profits, the third largest illicit industry after drugs and guns. Of the estimated 30 million people held in slavery around the world, as many as thirteen million of those are in India alone, and five million of those victims of slavery and indentured servitude are children.

In the United States there are an estimated two and a half million homeless children, 70,000 juveniles are incarcerated in youth detention facilities, and another 500,000 youth are brought to detention centers in a given year. 415,000 children are in foster care in the United States. Of the four million, and growing, Syrian refugees, it is estimated that more than half are children running away from war without a place to go. Palestinian youth in Gaza and the West Bank turn to violence because they cannot find a livelihood, own land, or marry.

In the Central American countries of El Salvador, Guatemala, and Honduras, where half the population lives below the poverty line, there are more than one million forgotten children who are trying to escape to the United States or other countries to find a better life. Many of those who don't escape, or who are forced to turn back, join drug cartels and gangs as their only means of livelihood and survival.

Between the ages of 10 and 13, I too experienced what it was like to be one of the runaway children held hostage by social prejudice and family violence. I was forced to run away to find my future. It's imperative that we do whatever we can to help children on the run—from war, violence, or abuse—to find safety and security.

GLOBAL GOAL 8

Decent Work and Economic Growth

Promote sustained, inclusive, and sustainable economic full and productive employment, and decent work for all

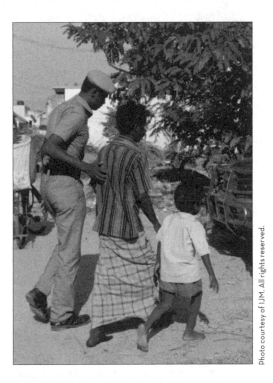

At 14 years old, Ragesh became a slave. Desperate to help his mother who was critically ill with tuberculosis, Ragesh took a loan from the owner of a mat-making business. He would use the money to buy medicine for his mother, and repay it through his labor. But that loan was a trap, and for 16 years Ragesh worked each day from 2:00 a.m. to 6:00 or 7:00 p.m. He was treated like machinery—no sick days, no switching tasks, and certainly no looking for another job.

Charities in Action

Free the Slaves liberates slaves, helps them rebuild their lives, and transforms the social, economic and political conditions that allow slavery to persist. We support community-driven interventions in partnership with local groups that help people to sustainable freedom and dismantle a region's system of slavery. We convince governments, international development organizations and businesses to implement key changes required for global eradication. We document and disseminate leading-edge practices to help the anti-slavery movement work more effectively. We raise awareness and promote action by opinion leaders, decision makers and the public. Free the Slaves is showing the world that ending slavery is possible.

ECPAT-USA fights for new and improved laws, encourages the private sector to do its part, and raises awareness among those who may be in a position to identify a child who is being commercially exploited.

IJM (International Justice Mission) collaborates with local authorities to rescue victims of slavery; bring traffickers and slave owners to justice; restore survivors to safety and strength; and strengthen the local justice system so it protects others from becoming victims.

CHAPTER SIX

Sequim—Land of Sunshine

The Indian meaning for Sequim is something like quiet waters, land of goodness. For me, it will always mean land of sunshine. It was a place where I could be a kid again and learn how to grow up—it was safe. The rich, fertile Dungeness river valley boasts the rugged, snowcapped Olympic Mountains on one side and the deep blue Strait of Juan de Fuca on the other, punctuated with the free-flowing Dungeness River, brimming with silvery flashes of wild salmon and Steelhead trout. Because Sequim sits in the rain shadow of the Olympic Mountains, the Sequim valley only receives an average of sixteen inches of measurable rainfall per year. The well-known farming land is only productive because of an irrigation system connecting the river to the rest of the Dungeness Valley.

I woke suddenly to the sound of voices that first morning back in Sequim. It was early in February 1971. The previous night, Mom and Jefferson had picked me up at the Seattle airport, and we'd driven the two hours back to Sequim, arriving around midnight. They didn't ask about how I ran away. I suppose it didn't matter at the time. What had been the most intense twenty-four hours of my life would, however, remain a lifetime memory for me. Through the years, my escape would grow in importance as I looked back and recalled the details, some better than others, and wondered what life would have been had I never run away from Dad.

I didn't recognize the voices coming from the other room. I was in my bedroom but it didn't really feel like home. We'd spent only a couple of months in this house before the judge had forced me to return to Kansas. The last time I'd slept here was the Sunday after Thanksgiving. The next day, I'd been picked up from school and sent to the detention center.

Mom swung open my door. A woman I'd never seen stood behind her. Mom introduced Nancy Schoessler and her five children, and they all came and stood by my bed. After the intense stress of the past two days, I couldn't handle it and exploded.

Coming into the small house with crooked doors, it was clear that it wasn't as grand as I'd remembered it. I realized this was not going to be easy. And then waking up to this family I didn't know set me off. I was an angry boy. I had first learned that by being mean, you could get your way. Then I learned that if you were angry, you could defend yourself. It was my first way of being. Without Jefferson, I would not have broken that cycle and would not have been able to choose being at peace inside.

"Get out. Get out!" I hollered.

Mom turned pale. The children scattered. Mom looked down at me, and I could see the pain etched on her face.

"So this is the one we've been shedding tears over," Mom's friend said. I had no idea who she was, but she already knew my entire story. The thought infuriated me. She turned and followed her kids out of my room.

I soon realized that Mom's days of keeping secrets were long gone; she had told all our private family matters to the Schoesslers. After years of hiding physical and emotional abuse, she was suddenly willing to share intimate family details with almost anyone. It was a change I found difficult to accept. Still, I regretted my child-scattering outburst almost immediately. Mom and Jefferson had made new friends. I might not know them yet, but these people cared about me. For the first time in years, we didn't need to hide anything. The change came swiftly and dramatically.

"You're going to have to be nicer than that," Mom said. She'd stayed beside my bed when the others left. I wanted to pull my head under the covers and disappear. "A lot of people all over Sequim shed tears for you. They prayed for you."

"Sorry," I said, throwing off my covers.

I smelled bacon sizzling. In the kitchen, I found Jefferson standing at the stove. He wore the same blue overalls he wore every workday. Today, he was cooking bacon and eggs before he left for work.

Looking around, I realized the house seemed smaller than I recalled. The red velvet wallpaper and turquoise walls and other decorative touches my mom had made when we moved in were still cheerful, but the rooms felt small. The front porch and utility room was home for Trixie and now one of her puppies who was blind at birth, Sleepy. There were prune trees in the back, which shaded the small yard. In the front stood the big wood pole barn, unpainted, at least three stories high for stacking and storing hay to feed the dairy cows in winter. The barn overshadowed the little white farmhouse with the turquoise shutters.

Surrounding the Port Williams house and barn were vast green hay fields as far as the eye could see, from all sides. In the distance the Olympic Mountains towered in the south, and to the north flowed the Strait of Juan de Fuca. In the gray morning light, Jefferson finished cooking, and the three of us sat at the kitchen table and ate breakfast together.

Three months earlier, we'd eaten Thanksgiving dinner at the same table. As she passed the bacon, Mom told me she and Jefferson had returned to the detention center and brought home Jerry, the American Indian boy who had been there with me. He'd stayed with them about a month before taking off for the reservation again.

I dropped my fork and knife and said, "How could you? How could you substitute another boy for me?"

"We didn't. You told us before you left the detention center that he needed help, so we brought him home."

"What if I came back? I would have had to live with Jerry."

Jefferson said, "It's okay, boy. He ran away again."

I was shocked. I recalled asking them to help him, but I didn't mean for them to bring him home. I felt betrayed and angry. They weren't supposed to replace me while I was gone. It was easy to be furious and resentful about Jerry. After all, he wasn't even nice to me when we were at the detention center. But deep down, I knew Jerry had it worse. He still didn't have a home or a family.

After breakfast, Jefferson went to work. He had taken a job to become a top hand for Maple View Dairy Farm. We had moved into our home at the Maple View Dairy farm, the next farm over from Graysmarsh, just before I had been taken away, so I hadn't had much chance to explore our new surroundings.

I took a walk outside. The Olympic Mountains rose above the lush green foothills. The Strait of Juan de Fuca separated Washington from Canada, and I thought about our ferry ride across the waterway the previous spring and wondered what would happen next. Would the judge send me back to Kansas yet again? Would I be allowed to stay with Mom and Jefferson? Would I ever get to live without worrying? Was it risky to get attached to this place once again?

I learned more about Mom and Jefferson's legal fight during my first days back in Sequim. A state appeals court had determined that the Kansas order giving Dad custody was unsupported by fact. According to the new ruling, the Kansas court failed to show any misconduct by Mom but instead made vague references to *"her association with black people."* So on January 14, 1971, while I languished at Tall Oaks, the Court of Appeals of the State of Washington reversed the order sending me back to Kansas. There was just one little problem, as I'd found out: The ruling held no weight, at least not in Kansas. Its enforceability required my presence in Washington, which meant my running away was not only full of risk but also legal.

At least, that's the way I looked at it. I never worried about seeing my dad again. My parents, especially my dad, had forced me to make a choice. I never looked back.

It also meant something else. Dad had kept custody of me in direct violation of the Washington State order. Even if he didn't need to abide by it, he certainly didn't tell me about it. In part, that explained why it was so important for him to intercept my mail. Had I learned about the appeals court's decision, I almost certainly would have done everything I could to get back to Sequim. As it turned out, all Dad needed to do to push me over the edge was tackle and punch me.

Back in Sequim, additional hearings would be held to determine my fate. Although the appeals court ruled in favor of Mom and Jefferson, it also ordered further litigation. In the meantime, I re-enrolled at Sequim Middle School. My classmates were shocked. Many of them had last seen me through the bulletproof glass of a police car, driving away from campus. In some ways, my return also surprised me. Looking out the patrol car window three months earlier, I didn't know if I'd ever see this place again. Now that I was back, school seemed the least of my concerns.

When Mom told me a trial date had been set, I was elated. The trial opened on Tuesday March 9, 1971. Brooke Taylor continued to serve as our attorney. For the first time I'd be allowed to testify, and I took off from school on Monday to prepare. My excitement soon waned. The judge heard testimony from two out-of-town witnesses who traveled to Sequim on our behalf. Grandma Hughes and Esther, a close friend of Mom's, were the only two allowed to take the stand. Esther would become an on-and-off-again lifelong friend and companion to Mom. After Esther graduated high school, she started her own beauty school in Bonner Springs where I would take my mom weekly to get her hair done. Esther always worried me because she smoked and didn't seem to be a good influence on my mom. But, again, she was another safe haven.

Esther told the court that dad regularly called Mom "a bitch or a whore." She also recalled the day Mom and I moved out of Tall Oaks. Esther had come over to help, and Dad stormed into the room and said Mom didn't need her. Then he turned to Esther and said, "Let me tell you one thing. What she needs is one last beating, and I'm going to give it to her if it's the last thing I do. She's going to be miserable the rest of her life."

Her testimony shocked me. I'd seen Dad hit Mom many times, but I never heard him speak like that. Esther also recalled how Mom would come to her house late at night. She described bite marks covering Mom's body and bruises on her neck. The worst time, she said, was when Mom had knife marks on her neck.

It was Esther's house that Mom had run to all those nights when I'd awakened to the sounds of violence. She often arrived at Esther's in tears. Looking back, I don't think I realized how bad the abuse had become. The thought of Dad holding a knife to Mom's throat brought me to tears. Mom and I had talked a bit about the abuse after their divorce when we lived by ourselves, but she never went into detail with me. She simply reached a point where she couldn't stand my father's meanness any longer, and so she left. She never dwelled on it and did not exactly think of herself as an abused woman. She felt they just couldn't live together because they were such different people, and she believed it was partly her fault. For years she had thought that she was supposed to stay because marriage vows were for life, and her parents never encouraged her to leave. Finally, she left because she understood that it was never going to get any better. She had to leave to survive.

During the two months I was back in Tall Oaks with Dad, Esther had tried to visit me five or six times. Dad never let her come close. Once, she knocked on the door at Tall Oaks and Dad verbally assaulted her, telling her she had no business coming around and claiming she was in a gang. Then he warned her to keep away.

Esther knew how bad things were between Dad and me. A few years earlier, she had witnessed an extreme emotional breakdown of mine following a weekend with Dad. When Mom couldn't calm me down, she called a doctor who gave me some medicine to relax.

Esther had also witnessed one of my recurring nightmares. Just before her testimony, she stayed with us in Sequim. That night I woke up screaming: "Don't let him take me! Don't let him take me! He'll get me." In the dream, I was looking out my bedroom window at Tall Oaks as Mom's Volkswagen bug sped away down the long gravel driveway; simultaneously, Dad pounded at the door, coming after Mom. His anger had reached across my bedroom, across the trundle bed, and out the window to snatch Mom out of the VW. I could never tell if she had gotten away, but the dream would almost always end with me shouting, "Take me with you!"

Grandma Hughes also testified about Dad's abuse and about my fear. She recalled watching Dad punch Mom and seeing bruises on Mom during her pregnancy. She said Dad had warned her to stay away when I was back at Tall Oaks. Once, he let me write a letter inviting my grandparents to visit. In the same envelope, Grandma said, Dad put a second letter. It told them not to come.

Grandma and Esther returned home to the Midwest shortly after their testimony. The rest of us didn't return to court until late July. During this time I remained with Mom and Jefferson in Sequim. With each passing month it began to feel more like home. Jefferson began to re-emerge as a preacher. He held a sunrise Easter service for a small group at Port Williams and regular Sunday services at American Legion Post 62.

As I settled back into life in Sequim, I realized something for the first time: We were poor. Near the end of the school year, when I was thirteen, Mom and Jefferson encouraged me to find a summer job. We needed the extra money. Mom didn't work, and Jefferson held a low-wage job with little opportunity for advancement. Mom motivated me by pointing out that I could pick berries if I didn't find anything else. The only problem was that jobs available to a thirteen-year-old were limited, even in a farming community.

I found my salvation at a local oyster farm. I worked early mornings on the tide flats. I'd been mesmerized by the Strait of Juan de Fuca since we arrived on the Olympic Peninsula. When I learned about the oyster job, it sounded perfect. I spent most mornings tending the flats, pulling large sacks from shallow water, placing mature oysters in huge buckets, seeding new beds, and otherwise helping out. If a menial task needed doing, I did it. And I loved every minute of it. Standing on the water, I could look north toward Canada and south at the snow-capped Olympic Mountains. In the morning light, it was hard to imagine a better place anywhere.

Jefferson left for work every weekday morning before five o'clock. Later, he also took a night job cleaning the Dungeness Inn. For his sermons at the Sequim American Legion Post 62 Jefferson made a pulpit out of plywood, and the small group that attended sat on folding chairs. Mom played piano. I had practically forgotten she knew how.

Word about Jefferson's preaching and singing spread slowly through Sequim. As we met more and more people, there was greater risk of being found.

My final custody hearing took place on July 29, 1971. The courthouse on Lincoln Street in Port Angeles stood just a few blocks from where Mom, Jefferson, and I spent our first night on the Olympic Peninsula. The historic brick building impressed and frightened me at the same time. I knew that whatever the judge decided would be final.

Mom, Jefferson, and I entered the courtroom together. Dark wooden bench seats with high backs filled most of the room. A line of windows running along the south wall admitted bright light from outside. Two banisters separated the front of the room from the rest, and two tables sat opposite each other in front of the judge's bench with a space mimicking an aisle between them.

I sat in front on one side with Mom and Jefferson. Dad sat with his attorney at the table across from us. Two large flags—the Stars and Stripes and the green Washington State flag with a picture of George Washington—bracketed the judge's bench. The same dark wood that paneled the bench seats behind us also decorated the judge's bench and the wall behind him. The wall's heavy varnish reflected the light from outside.

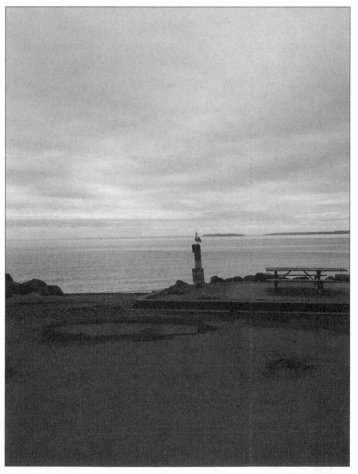

Port Williams

Some of the members of Jefferson's church filed into the public viewing area. So did others from the Sequim community. Looking behind us, I saw some of my classmates and their families.

As the proceedings began, part of me wanted to stand up and tell everyone about Dad's abuse—about how he'd beaten Mom, about how I watched him strangle her, hit her, and throw her to the ground. Memories rushed over me, and I couldn't help but think about the old house in Edwardsville. For a moment, I forgot about the violence and saw myself standing in the front yard after a snowstorm. It always seemed so peaceful right after a fresh snow, surrounded by whiteness and quiet in the gap of silence between passing trains. As a little boy, never did I feel as safe as when I went outside to play in the snow.

The hearing lasted two days. Dad's attorney argued that Jefferson was unfit to raise me. Rather than base his case on race—we weren't in Kansas anymore, after all—he argued that Jefferson's lack of a high school diploma made him unfit to be a father. He also dug up old rumors about Mom having a romantic relationship with a black student at Bonner Springs High.

The judge accepted witness testimony given in Kansas. A handful of people spoke on Dad's behalf. Each talked about his strong community standing, his skills as a pastor, and his leadership as a camp counselor. One of the witnesses had attended Phillips University with Mom and Dad. Another met them shortly after we moved to Edwardsville. One of them called Mom a "controversial woman" and said she "would give special attention to colored children and carry on with them." Another witness said Mom was responsible for the "weakening of the faith of a great many people."

Brooke Taylor fought back with witnesses who spoke about Dad's abuse and about my fear of my father. He also called on Sequim community members, who talked about our family and about Jefferson's paternal character. On the second day of the hearing, the judge called me to the stand. For the first time in fourteen years, I spoke openly and on the record about the abuse I'd grown up with.

At one point, he asked the question I had long wanted to answer in front of a judge.

"Who do you want to live with, Scottie?"

I didn't hesitate. "My mom and Jefferson."

Dad stared at me from a few feet away.

Before I stepped down, I made one final plea: "Please don't send me back to Kansas."

My time on the stand passed quickly. The courtroom remained silent as I stepped down and sat beside Mom and Jefferson. Shortly afterward, the judge dismissed us. Before he did, he said he'd review the evidence and testimony and make his decision in a few days.

I was shocked. What else did he need to hear? Why couldn't he just say we won and send Dad back to Kansas? I walked out of the courtroom feeling uneasy. Dad approached me in the hallway. I began to tremble as he spoke.

"No matter what happens, I want you to know I love you," he said.

I froze. We hadn't talked since the night I ran away. I couldn't remember ever hearing him say those words before. I didn't know what to do. Before I could speak, Mom stepped to my side, said good-bye, and led me down the hall.

On August 6, 1971, Judge Joseph H. Johnston awarded my care, custody, and control to Mom. In addition, the court recognized my affection for Jefferson and noted that he, Mom, and I shared "a relationship of mutual affection, trust, and respect."

The judge noted my fear of my father and called out the Kansas court for taking me away from Mom without reason. Then, citing geographical reality and our deteriorating relationship, the judge stripped Dad of all legal visitation rights. He assigned a mediator to help us discuss the possibility of future visits, but neither one of us ever followed up.

In the four decades since Judge Johnston's decision, I have many times wondered how my life would have turned out had he ruled the other way.

During the rest of my time in Sequim, Dad never called or wrote a letter to me. Three and a half years after the custody ruling, Jefferson and I returned to the courthouse and changed my legal name to Scott Jackson. I never called my biological father Dad again.

By September of 1972, Jefferson's little congregation at the American Legion post was flourishing. When a local Methodist church put its building up for sale, Jefferson's parishioners pooled fifteen hundred dollars and bought it. They called it the Little Brown Church of Blyn, taking the title from the song "The Church in the Wildwood."

The building was one room with a small walled-off kitchen. As the congregation grew, we added extensions for Sunday school and social events. The church thrived in those early years. Jefferson never accepted a salary, and he never wrote a sermon. He preached the words God gave him, and he never ran out of things to say. His most popular sermon each year came on Easter when the congregation and a large number of guests gathered at the beach at nearby Port Williams. Jefferson saw Easter as an opportunity to baptize as many people as he could in the cold saltwater. I recall standing on the sand and watching him dunk newcomers while he stood waist deep off the beach in the morning light.

We also hosted an annual pig roast. Each summer, we buried a pig and let it cook through the night. The following day, always a Sunday, we dug up the meat after church. Christian or not, people came from all around to taste that pork, considered by many to be the Olympic Peninsula's best.

Our live nativity scene also brought the crowds. Each year, we welcomed live farm animals to the property in front of the church. Adults and children from the congregation joined them in an impressive re-creation of the first Christmas. Mom spent each fall sewing costumes for everyone who participated, including me. The best years were those when a new baby joined the congregation, giving us a live actor for the role of baby Jesus.

If Jefferson was the Little Brown Church's shepherd, Mom was its leading lady, musical influence, and lead social planner. Much like she had done back in Edwardsville, she embraced her role as pastor's wife. She played the piano each Sunday, helped anyone who needed it, and made sure no church event lacked a proper celebration, however big or small.

Reverend Pat Wright began to bring her Total Experience Children's Choir from Seattle to the Little Brown Church. Wright had arrived in Seattle in 1974 and grown into the city's first lady of gospel music. The Little Brown Church was the first place she brought the choir outside of Seattle so they could sing with Jefferson. There was always a packed church when they visited. Soon after, the rumors started to fly. The Sequim townspeople worried that blacks from the Seattle central district were going to move over and camp out on the Little Brown Church grounds. Fortunately, that rumor finally got squashed.

Our family was always a novelty. Jefferson embraced it. He met every store owner, every waitress, every child, all with a smile. There was no one he met that he didn't like. In turn, they had to like Jefferson. He was a farmer just like them. The Pacific Northwest was different. Vancouver, British Columbia, was an especially international community—there just weren't many African Americans. But we couldn't stay in Vancouver. In Port Angeles, there were difficulties with getting a taxi or a hotel room and plenty of stares. But from the day we drove the Studebaker to Sequim, it was a more accepting place.

The man on the Coho Ferry was right—people from all over the world were settling in Sequim. Yes, it was the beginning of the retirees' influx, but also writers, artists, and hippies were all mixing with traditional dairy farmers and the berry farmers, which predated today's lavender farms. Still, other than the Schoessler family, we didn't receive many invitations to dinner from anyone in Sequim.

Jefferson never showed it, but he knew what I knew—that there were some places neither he nor our family would be invited.

Jefferson's preaching and singing continued to inspire me as much as they had that first day back at Gethsemane Baptist. As we continued to make ourselves a home in Sequim, nowhere did I feel more at peace than sitting in the pews of the Little Brown Church.

The first couple of years back in Sequim were not always easy for me. I spent a good part of the time testing my mom and Jefferson. I questioned school; I questioned the two of them. I angrily questioned Jefferson and sometimes challenged his authority. But the few times that I tried to take out our circumstances on my mom, Jefferson would intervene. One of our worst experiences was when I talked back to my mom, and he asked me to stop. I wouldn't, and we wound up wrestling through the kitchen. I said words I shouldn't have. Jefferson smacked me across the cheek or shoulder, but it was more about getting me to shut up. He was so strong that he knocked me across the room into my drum set. Whenever he would tell me to stop talking back or yelling at my mom, I would then react to him.

"Boy, you got to stop talking back to your mom and be nice to her."

"But she isn't nice to me."

"It doesn't matter, Boy. She's your mom and you are the child, so you have to obey her."

"But she's wrong."

"It doesn't matter. Boy, I don't care what you call me, but you are not going to call your mother names in front of me."

During this time I also struggled to find my way in school, but Jefferson encouraged me. I remember sitting at our little kitchen table at night. The room's single overhead lamp cast a yellow circle of light on my homework. Jefferson sat with me, doing his best, with his limited education, to help me.

One afternoon I accidentally let the pig out of the pen. Jefferson took his shotgun outside and fired it into the air, just meaning to scare the pig. We all watched it fall dead. My mom was so angry and in tears at the same time. She started screaming at Jefferson. This time, he'd had enough. Mom kept screaming and he finally just walked out of the house, climbed into his green Dodge truck, and drove away. He didn't come back for hours.

Mom and I began to wonder if he would ever return. We couldn't blame him. After all, although a terrible thing had happened, there were a lot more important things in our life than the loss of the pig. After dark, Jefferson made his way back. He didn't come inside; he made a fire outside near the pole barn and heated some water. He dressed the pig and I went and watched him. Mom came out and joined us. We had survived together, and it didn't make sense to fall apart now. That night, I understood some of the sacrifices that Jefferson had made to be here in Sequim, without his extended family, without anyone else he knew—just to be with the two of us.

Jefferson and I became closer during these years, too. When I began to question my faith and Christianity during high school, Jefferson supported my searching. He listened patiently and encouraged me as I read other religious works, including sections of the Koran and writings about the Kabbalah. Through it all, Jefferson pointed to what he saw as Christianity's two most important principles: forgiveness and redemption.

We often had conversations in the evening around nine or ten o'clock, when we would be in the kitchen together. I would just be getting to my homework, and he would be getting ready to go to bed.

"Jefferson, I've now read the Koran, and I've studied Buddhism and Hinduism, and read the Bible all the way through, and I still believe in God. But what I don't know is what's different about the Christian faith compared to all these other faiths. They also seem important, so why Christianity instead of these other faiths?"

"Boy, none of those faiths are bad. It's more important how you live your life. Even people without faith can live a godly life just by being good to others. The reason I believe in Christianity is because we can all be forgiven no matter what we've done, and I'm not perfect."

These conversations were as much about forgiving myself as accepting my faith. I always thought that I was less than perfect, that I wasn't worthy. Because of the way I grew up, maybe my mom and I had done something to deserve all this. I never really forgave myself. But through Jefferson, I began to see that I was worthy and, more important, could choose to do something meaningful with my life.

Planning for Sustainability

Sequim, Washington, where we ran away to and where I grew up, is a place of natural beauty. Nestled between the snowcapped Olympic Mountains and the Strait of Juan de Fuca, the Sequim valley has grown from two thousand people when I first lived there to more than twenty thousand people, and it now boasts a Walmart, Target, McDonalds, and $1 million dollar homes dotting the hillside once covered in magnificent Douglas fir and cedar trees, reaching to the mountains and clear blue sky above.

The Dungeness River, where fewer and fewer salmon and steelhead spawn, is still a pristine wilderness river. I had the good fortune to help support the Sequim community's efforts to take back a portion of their farmland and reclaim it for what is now the second largest lavender growing and harvesting region in the world after the Provence region in France.

The Sequim lavender festival brings in ten thousand people a year, with a booming tourist trade year round. Sequim is still home to its own herd of elk and other wildlife, including brown bears, cougars, and wolves. President Roosevelt, when he visited the Olympic Peninsula, declared it a national treasure and established an Olympic National Park.

Yet 2015 and 2016 are the warmest years in the 137-year recording of our planet's average surface temperature. There have been more natural disasters associated with climate change in the past 30 years than in all of recent history. We refuse to believe we are in a global environmental crisis. The Global Goals for Sustainability and the Global Climate Compact give us an opportunity to change all that for generations to come. We can and must restore the earth and honor the respective country and global commitments that have been made to reduce carbon and greenhouse gas emissions; implement large-scale reforestation

115

and restore vital water sheds; preserve and replenish valuable farm-land with adequate water; and protect our oceans and sea life. We must commit to new sources of renewable, clean energy and storage and distribution of electrical power for those countries and communities that currently do not have access to or do not have reliable sources of electrical power.

Currently thirteen million people live on depleted, untillable land. One billion have no access to electricity, and three billion rely on bio mass fuels, such as wood, charcoal, and coal, emitting dangerous carbons to fuel their homes and wood stoves.

Global Impact works closely with Restore the Earth Foundation, which has developed a social impact model that is proven to significantly reduce carbons, provide economic development, and offer measurable community benefits through large-scale land restoration and reforestation.

Startup companies like CleanSpark, another Global Impact partner, produce cost-effective technologies to store, manage, and distribute micro grid energy from clean alternative sources. Corporations like Gap and Walmart and many others have now made commitments to reduce their footprint and protect the earth. It is not just about preserving the natural beauty of my hometown of Sequim; it is about saving all of our countries and fulfilling the Global Goals for Sustainability essential to preserving our resources, protecting our climate, and restoring the earth for generations to come.

| 12 RESPONSIBLE CONSUMPTION AND PRODUCTION | 13 CLIMATE ACTION | 14 LIFE BELOW WATER | 15 LIFE ON LAND |

GLOBAL GOALS 12, 13, 14, and 15

- *Ensure sustainable consumption and production patterns*
- *Take urgent action to combat climate change and its impacts*
- *Conserve and sustainably use the oceans, seas, and marine resources for sustainable development*
- *Protect, restore, and promote sustainable use of terrestrial ecosystems, sustainably manage forests, combat desertification, and halt and reverse land degradation and halt biodiversity loss*

In Bolivia's Amazon forests are wild cacao trees that have been cared for by indigenous peoples for centuries. Each year between January and March, Abraham Noza and his village harvest what they need and sell the surplus. Since ancient times the indigenous peoples have had cocoa as one of their main food and income sources; however, the pressure on land, expansion of the agricultural frontier, and illegal exploitation of natural resources threatens their primary way of life. For people like Abraham, it is a challenge not just to maintain sustainable natural resources but to protect their livelihoods by protecting the trees that generate income.

117

Charities in Action

One of Heifer International's most important promises is to care for the Earth. For development to be sustainable, Heifer helps families raise their livestock in harmony with nature.

⬤ Restore the Earth
FOUNDATION

REF's mission is to restore the Earth's essential forest and wetland ecosystems. REF currently works on one of the largest landscape-scale restoration projects in North America: one million acres of critical land in the Mississippi River Basin.

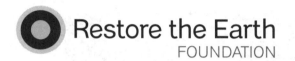

PCI Media Impact works in over 60 countries to bring about social change in the fields of public health, environment, human rights and social justice. They are changing the world one story at a time.

CHAPTER SEVEN

Making My Way

Not long after the final custody trial, Mom and Jefferson announced their plan to adopt a child. I was shocked and a little jealous after everything we had been through. For the first time in years, I felt like everything was going great. Why in the world would they want another child? More selfishly, why didn't they want to focus on me? After all, it was hard enough. We were poor.

They applied for adoption and requested a newborn of mixed race. When the news came a few months later, it seemed like a dream. Somewhere in Eastern Washington in the city of Spokane— which seemed just as unfamiliar as Sequim did when we first arrived there—seven hours away, a little girl was waiting for her new parents. Mom and Jefferson left the next day by bus. When they returned two days later, I was a big brother. I had used part of my paycheck to pay for a white snowsuit for the baby, and they brought her home in it. They introduced me to Jeffie-Lou Jackson, named after Jefferson and Sydney-Lou. I thought, *Who in the world would name their daughter Jeffie-Lou?* Nonetheless, it was one of the happiest days of my life. I fell in love with my litter sister the moment I saw her. She was a cherub, with fat dimpled cheeks on both sides. Mom dressed her in a blue bonnet. She wasn't happy about it either. Her skin was a beautiful shade of mocha, and she had dark brown soft loose curls everywhere. I loved her at first sight.

Thanks to mom's sewing, taste, and style, Jeffie-Lou grew up the most boldly dressed child on our side of Puget Sound. She quickly became the center of our world. She was dynamic and beautiful, and she filled our home with a new sense of joy and purpose. Then came another surprise. A few months after Jeffie-Lou joined our family, we received a call. Shawne Hosea was three years old. He had already been through a series of foster homes and now needed a new place to live. Like Jeffie-Lou, he was of mixed race. Several families had wanted to adopt him but couldn't afford his medical bills. Shawne had severe allergies and asthma and required an expensive regimen of medication. He joined our family as a foster child. That was the only way the state would pay his medical expenses. For Mom and Jefferson, that wasn't good enough.

When Mom read a news story about a doctor in Seattle who had experienced a similar issue and was awarded medical support from the legislature, she sped into action. An occasional parishioner from the Little Brown Church served in state government as our state

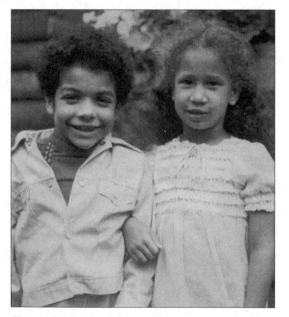

Shawne and Jeffie-Lou

legislator and helped Mom learn more. After many phone calls and a stack of paperwork, we were accepted into the new program. We adopted Shawne soon afterward.

Shawne and I shared a bedroom. At night, he'd wake up screaming and gasping for air. I'd rush to his side to help. Many times, I thought we were going to lose him. As his medical problems continued, so did our worries. I learned to stay up late and operate on a few hours of sleep. It was the best way to make sure I would be ready if anything went wrong. Perhaps in helping to take care of Shawne and Jeffie-Lou, I learned to put aside myself in favor of others.

Mom tried desperately to improve Shawne's health. She altered his diet, changed his medicines, and threw away everything she thought might cause an allergic reaction. She made sure his inhalers and prescriptions were close at all times. We even sent him to Denver, when he was older, to see the top respiratory doctors in the country. By the time he left, doctors said he was likely getting as good care at home as he could in a hospital.

Mom encouraged me to take a speech class my first year in high school. She then helped me write speeches and with the support of the Speech and Debate Club coach, who believed I had potential, I began to win every competition. Grandma Hughes was proud too, even if my speeches weren't sermons. My specialty was like a sermon—the long oratory. It had to be ten minutes long, recited from memory, and an original work. After school, when no one was around, I would stand in front of the only full-length mirror in our little house and practice my oration and delivery. Sometimes, I would catch myself embracing the words and other times, I would imagine, as I looked into the mirror, that my words would have an impact on others.

The speech that took me all the way to the state championship was about bondage and prejudice. I started it by singing a few lines of the Russian slave song, "Yo, heave ho!" I was awarded first place in the regional competition, and my coach and I were the only ones from Sequim traveling across the state to Ellensburg for the Washington State Speech and Debate Competition. I remember the coach driving down Highway 101 on the descent to the Hood Canal Bridge. You could see the Olympic Mountains and the sparkling blue water of Hood Canal. I knew I was supposed to be here.

After each round, my name was called to compete in the next round. Then the final round arrived. We didn't know what to think. The other two students had done a great job, and I had done my best, delivering my speech flawlessly. When the time came for them to announce the State Champion in each category, they saved oratory for last. Sure enough, they called my name. Sequim High School displayed my trophy. It was amazing. The very issue that had brought me to Sequim and turned our lives upside down was now the subject of my winning oratory: "No one should be kept from realizing their full potential because of the limitations of others." When we returned to Sequim, it was past midnight. I woke up my parents. They weren't as excited to be awakened as I was to tell them the news. Regardless, it was a great accomplishment.

I became more confident in myself. I was starting to enjoy school and excel in my schoolwork. I even wanted to play sports, especially basketball, but instead I applied for a job at Southwoods, the Sequim Country dry goods store, and was hired. I needed my after-school job. It gave me independence. Some weeks, I earned as much money as my parents did. Southwoods was owned by Chuck and Howard. Many in Sequim said they were a couple, but they were my friends and mentors, and I didn't care. They taught me how to eat escargot and made sure I had nice clothes to wear. They also owned the Town and Country clothing store across the street from Southwoods, and sometimes they would have me model the clothes for the local newspaper ads.

Working there wasn't always fun and games. There were fourteen older women who served as clerks under Chuck and Howard. At first

I thought I knew it all, especially how to sweep the floors and take out the trash. I would do everything as quickly as I could, not paying attention that I wasn't always taking the time to do a good job. The clerks started complaining that I was too sloppy and careless, quick to get the job done but not careful enough to do it well. Chuck and Howard would not have this. One evening, they took me aside and let me know that they would have to fire me if I didn't learn to do a complete job. I was caught off guard, but I learned quickly a deeper sense of humility. I learned to do my best regardless of the task. I soon became the best sweeper of floors and even cleaned the toilets, and the clerks never complained again. Instead they finally got together with Chuck and Howard and welcomed me into the Southwoods close-knit family.

During my junior year of high school, my peers started calling me "Action Jackson" and elected me student body president. Just as I was finally feeling accepted and like I belonged, my mother pushed me out of my comfort zone and insisted that I apply for a Rotary international exchange program. She felt strongly—much more than I did—that if I got the chance to travel as an international exchange student, it would be the experience of a lifetime. She knew that I was young for my class, so it wouldn't hurt to enter college a year later. She also understood that we didn't necessarily have the means for me to attend college. After the interviews, I didn't think much more about the application. Then, one dark, wet, and cold December evening, Mom and I arrived home at the same time, and she picked up the mail from the mailbox and followed me in the door near the plum trees.

"Scottie," she leaped, "you got it! You've been accepted as a Rotary exchange student to New Zealand."

"What? When?" I asked, not even hearing or caring about the choice of country.

"When do they want me to go?" I repeated.

"They want you to leave January 12th in time for the beginning of the school year Down Under."

There was a sinking feeling in my stomach.

"I can't go," I blurted out.

"You can't *not* go," she replied. My mom was emphatic. "You are not going to lose the chance of a lifetime to see the world."

"We'll see," I said. "I told them on the application I couldn't go until after the school year. Maybe I could appeal."

But Rotary only had the one placement. I had to take the opportunity or give it to the next student. Jefferson thought I should go, but not as strongly as Mom. Everyone at school thought I should go, even the teachers, and especially the principal as he was a Rotarian and had been my sponsor for the application. *But what about graduation?* I thought. I couldn't bear the thought of coming back and having to go through one more semester to graduate. I wouldn't be student body president and the few friends I had would be gone. I only had one class left: American history.

The teachers devised a plan whereby if I read the textbook and then successfully passed both a written and oral exam, I would be allowed to graduate in absentia with my class.

Even Howard and Chuck of Southwoods agreed that I should go. They bought my luggage and made sure that I had new clothes to take with me. I passed the exams, packed my bags, and said my goodbyes. Suddenly, I was headed to New Zealand whether I wanted to or not.

I left in January, reluctantly, abdicating my position as student body president and finishing my high school degree six months early. The Sunday before I left, I sat in the front of the Little Brown Church and listened to Jefferson preach. I remember the congregation singing "Love Lifted Me." The refrain struck me as particularly beautiful on this day.

> *Love lifted me!*
> *Love lifted me!*
> *When nothing else could help,*
> *Love lifted me!*

The sun seemed to shine brighter than usual for January. I remember how warm it felt on my arm through the church windows. Jefferson was preaching with extra emotion. Mom played the piano, and Jeffie-Lou and Shawne, my adopted sister and brother, sat next to me in the front pew. The church was packed. Jefferson always preached from scripture. I especially liked to hear him preach on the 23rd Psalm. The words came to him with ease.

> *The Lord is my shepherd, I shall not be in want.*
> *He makes me lie down in green pastures,*
> *He leads me beside quiet waters,*
> *He restores my soul.*

Listening to him, I thought about everything we had been through since that day we first met at Gethsemane Baptist. As the service winded down, Jefferson looked right at me.

"This is a special day," he said. "Scottie, our number one son, is leaving tomorrow. Come up here, son. We are all very proud of you."

I didn't want to go away again, even to New Zealand. I was just learning how to belong. As Jefferson spoke of how proud he was, I thought, *Don't they want me here? Why is everyone so happy I'm leaving?*

I had no idea this was going to happen.

"We want you to say a few words before you go."

I didn't know what to say, so I spoke from the heart.

"Thank you. You all have meant everything to me. When we arrived in Sequim, we didn't know anyone. Now I feel like I'm leaving behind more than I could ever have imagined. You stood beside us when it mattered most. Without you, the Little Brown church, and your faith in me and my family, none of this would have been possible."

When I started to walk back down from the pulpit to the pew, Mom spoke up. "Scottie, we want you to play our song."

I returned to the piano. My mother loved this song because I had written it for her when just the two of us had lived in our trailer on the Edwardsville farm. I had written it from the heart and to avoid piano practice. I began to play. There were many chords in my song, and then I started to sing.

> *When I was little, my mother used to sit me on her lap.*
> *She would read me the stories of the Bible and I used to love*
> *them so very much.*

Six months later, my parents called long distance to New Zealand to report that Jefferson had been asked to give the high school graduation invocation and receive my diploma. It was the only high school diploma Jefferson would ever receive, even if it was mine.

Jefferson had never received a high school diploma because he had left school to work full time on the farm before he finished the tenth grade, at least two years short of being able to graduate. So when he was asked to give the invocation for the Sequim High School graduation that year and receive my diploma in my absence, it was a big deal.

Afterward people in Sequim said it was one of the most meaningful invocations ever at graduation. Jefferson of course was the only person of color either on stage or in the audience. But we were used to that by now. Knowing that Jefferson and Mom were there, even though I wasn't, made it seem a little better. Jefferson was proud of me and I was proud of him. I was thousands of miles away in New Zealand, but we were still connected. In fact, I always felt connected to Jefferson no matter what the circumstances. It was something I could count on and perhaps a feeling I only had with two other people—but in different ways—Mom and Grandpa Whitey.

My year in New Zealand introduced me to the world and left a lasting impression on me. New Zealanders talked funny and drove on the wrong side of the road. We wore uniforms to school. I went to Rotary meetings every week, which always started with everyone standing and singing "God Save the Queen." I lived with four different host families, including a Maori family. The Maori people of Polynesian descent were the first people to inhabit New Zealand. I recognized for the first time that the gap between rich and poor didn't just exist in the United States but around the world. I learned there are good people everywhere in the world regardless of race, religion, or culture, willing to help others.

In New Zealand I was another white person in a predominately white society. It was easy to fit in. But when I lived with my Maori host family, I was reminded once again of the impact of race. My Maori mother watched over me and even taught me how to drive on the wrong side of the road, until we both learned that Rotary had an international policy prohibiting exchange students from driving. One day my Maori host father informed me that his sister had died and that he wanted me to come with them to the family wake.

The wake lasted three days and was held in a long house where we mourned with the body. The front entrance to the long house was decorated in Maori traditional motif with a very small opening. Statuesque totem poles surrounded the house, which had a series of masks carved into the wood. The roofline was an A-frame with beams pointing down, and the roof boards had the classic Polynesian curved motif. We had to stoop down to get inside, but then we were able to stand up again. Once we entered, it was clear that the structure extended back considerably. On each side of the house was a long, built-in bench with carvings on both sides. Each side of the house had cots and mats where we would sleep. The body was placed at the far end in an open casket like a shroud in a wooden holder, resembling a manger.

Mid-morning of the third and final day, we left the long house and walked across the gravel road to the local pub. At first, it was only the mourning party, and I was the only nonfamily member. Then the community members began to filter into the pub and join the celebration. Tables started to fill; bar stools had two and three deep. The air was filled with a mixture of laughter, tears, and memories. The bar served draft and tap beer at room temperature. We slept in the long house again that night. After a final full day and night of celebration for a woman I had only met after she died, the casket was finally closed and my Maori host father's sister could now rest in peace.

My year Down Under came to an end too quickly. What remained were a broader point of view and a greater understanding of cultural differences and perspectives. For the first time, I understood that there were kids like me around the world who experienced similar prejudices and struggles.

I went home to face the challenges of being in Sequim and to find my way forward.

While I was away in New Zealand, Jefferson and Mom bought five acres in the woods. After picking me up from the Seattle airport, we returned to the log cabin they had literally built with their own hands. Two stained glass windows with the words "God is Love" and "Love Thy Neighbor" reflected the labor of love it took to build the cabin. The cabin was deep in the woods, halfway up Lost Mountain Road.

As I walked up to the cabin for the first time, I couldn't help but be amazed. It was a remarkable sight. The cedar logs had come from the property and had been milled nearby at one of the portable mills in the area. This is where they smoothed the two sides of the log that would be stacked atop each other and left the rounded sides for facing inside and outside. The cabin was huge and even larger once you were inside. Jefferson had taken a string to measure how large the cabin would be, and he kept expanding the string, not sure it looked big enough.

It was an open loft design. The bedrooms were all on the loft level, except for the one guest bedroom. There were no doors to the

The log cabin

bedrooms. The balcony railing separated the bedrooms from the expansive first floor below. The railing and the stairs leading to the second level loft were made from the same rough-cut logs milled from the property. The ceiling was thirty feet high, which added to the sense of expansiveness when you looked down from the balcony to the kitchen, dining room, and living room. Those rooms were appointed with faux oriental rugs over the Douglas fir planks, which made up the floor. Antique wood stoves were placed throughout the cabin. A paper maché zebra nestled in one corner, mother's colorful hats and dolls in another. The sixteen-foot-high china cabinet mom bought with my tax return from working at Southwoods while I was in New Zealand was in another corner.

Sydney and Jefferson had made a home that was uniquely ours. They explained they had made sure to carefully place letters they had received from me when I was taken back to Kansas along with a picture of me in a small memory box that was under the cornerstone of the cabin. In this way, the reasons why we were here amongst the cedar and fir trees would never be forgotten. The Schoesslers gave us a North American Chestnut tree, which was carefully planted in the front yard.

The log cabin served as yet another anchor, together with the Little Brown Church, to remind me that we had found a home. I was in awe of what Mom and Jefferson had accomplished in a year while I was gone. I was also afraid that after all I had achieved before I had left for the exchange year, I was back to where I started—without a foreseeable future.

Accessing Good Health Care and Nutrition

When I was first recruited by Dr. Chris Elias, then President and CEO of PATH, my passion was centered more on the needs of children and youth, whose issues I could relate to because of my own childhood experience with meningitis and my brother Shawne's severe health issues. But I soon learned that access to good health is a fundamental right and a building block for global development. Pursuing Global Health is not about us and them. Pandemics such as HIV AIDS, Malaria, SARS, Ebola, and the Zika outbreak affect all of us, countries rich or poor.

PATH is one of the largest grantees of the Bill & Melinda Gates Foundation and is committed to bringing low-cost health technologies and vaccines to those without access to such solutions. Chris Elias now serves as President of Global Development for the Bill & Melinda Gates Foundation, where he plays a leadership role in a fight we are winning to eradicate polio. While at PATH, I was involved in supporting the PATH teams working for malaria elimination and the delivery of a new low-cost vaccine (Menafrivac) to prevent meningitis A in twenty-six of the poorest countries in Africa, where meningitis A infections have caused havoc on their respective victims, leaving them paralyzed and/or debilitated.

Early in my tenure with World Vision, I was called into action to join the fight against HIV AIDS. In 2000, Rich Stearns, then the newly appointed President of World Vision U.S., took his first trip to Africa. There he witnessed firsthand the devastating effects HIV AIDS was having on Sub-Saharan Africa. Our own World Vision staff members were dying of AIDS, and more than 10 million orphans had lost one or both of their parents to AIDS. HIV AIDS was no longer a disease infecting only men or intravenous drug users.

Today more than 60 percent of those living with AIDS world-wide are women. Rich came back with his heart broken, committed to raising awareness and funds to ensure that history would not look back on our generation as the one responsible for the HIV AIDS global pandemic. Yet, in a recent survey, less than 6 percent of World Vision donors, child sponsors, or the American church community at large were willing to support HIV AIDS orphans, let alone those being infected with the disease.

With limited resources, we set in motion the HIV AIDS Hope Tour. We traveled to twenty-one cities, meeting with church leaders, the media, and World Vision donors, calling upon all of them to engage in the fight against HIV AIDS. We joined forces with many others and supported President Bush's unprecedented commitment to PEPFAR, the President's Emergency Plan for AIDS Relief—the largest single development commitment by the United States since the Marshall plan to support Europe following World War II. We applauded efforts by former President Clinton and the Clinton Foundation to negotiate affordable pricing between the affected countries and the drug companies providing access to antiretroviral virus drugs (ARVS), essential to keeping alive those who have been infected.

We now have new tools to stop the transmission of HIV from mother to child, and many more of those infected are living productive lives. Overall infections are down, and we are indeed on our way to winning the war against HIV AIDS. But we can't let down our guard, because we have yet to find a vaccine or cure for HIV. We must continue this fight against the global threat of infectious and non-infectious diseases if we are to fulfill the promise of the Global Goals of making health accessible for everyone. We must train health workers on the front lines and establish health systems that will protect us from outbreaks, such as Ebola, which was the cause of 1,000 deaths in West Africa and severely impacted the people and marginal health systems of Liberia, Sierra Leone, and West Guinea.

Now we are battling the Zika virus, caused by mosquitoes carrying the virus, which is currently estimated to infect more than four million people in Latin America and around the world. It has been linked to causing microcephaly in infants of infected pregnant women, resulting in abnormally small heads with adverse development of those affected.

Every year, Malaria continues to infect more than 200 million people and accounts for over half a million deaths, mostly children. Forty percent of the world's children live in a country where there is the threat of malaria, which can now be prevented with a ten-dollar bed net to keep them safe at night, as long as they receive adequate donations.

Six million children under the age of five die from preventable causes *every year*. More than 150 million living are malnourished. For as many as 2.6 million children who die, malnutrition is an underlying cause. Forty million women give birth without a trained health worker by their side. For every one thousand babies born, 172 die from a lack of access to basic health care. Even when children don't die in their first one thousand days, they can be affected by blindness, stunting, and mental or physical development issues.

At Global Impact we provide support services to the Global Health Council, comprised of more than 400 members, implementing programs and advocating for access to good health and nutrition. There are many members of our Global Impact alliance who are on the front lines, including Doctors Without Borders (MSF), UNICEF, PATH, MSH, International Medical Corps, Direct Relief, Americare, and many more. We must remain vigilant in order to ensure that everyone on the planet has access to good health.

3 GOOD HEALTH AND WELL-BEING

GLOBAL GOAL 3

Good Health and Well-Being

Ensure healthy lives and promote well-being for all at all ages

Nina received vital nutrition services and treatment for tuberculosis from International Medical Corps.

One-year-old Nina was malnourished and underweight, a condition exacerbated by the fact that she also had tuberculosis. Tragically, Nina's story is far from uncommon in coastal Kenya, where about 50 percent of the population lives below the poverty line. Nina's grandmother took her to a new program to address the high levels of underweight children in the region. Thirty-two underweight children, including Nina, and their caregivers started in the program to learn about locally available nutritious foods and the importance of a varied diet. In addition to starting her on a program to help her reach a target weight, health workers also put Nina on treatment for tuberculosis. After, Nina weighed 18 pounds, a much healthier weight for a one-year-old baby.

Charities in Action

International Medical Corps

Medical Corps focuses on the delivery of community-based primary health care, with an emphasis on training and education, and hiring of local staff.

Amref Health Africa increases immunization coverage for common childhood diseases, promotes family planning, improves infant and child nutrition practices, and increases access to care.

PATH develops and introduces affordable drugs for diseases that disproportionately affect people in low-income countries, including drugs to treat or prevent newborn infections, malaria, and HIV.

CHAPTER EIGHT

Where Are
the Scholarships?

I was determined to go to an Ivy League school—or at least one with ivy-covered brick buildings. My mom was more realistic and encouraged me to work and attend a nearby community college. Despite my success as an international student, I returned from New Zealand without a single college scholarship. I had spent hours completing applications before I left, but Mom told me she had never mailed any of them, including the final submissions to Harvard and the University of Chicago, where I was pursuing small school talent criteria. Mom explained that we couldn't afford the difference in what we would still have had to pay for tuition even with financial aid. I was devastated. For the first time in my life, I felt like she had let me down.

Instead of the Ivy League, I found a job at a nearby plywood mill to save for a more substantial school. Howard and Chuck were willing to let me work at Southwoods again, but I wouldn't earn enough there to pay for a four-year college. They then used their connections to get me an interview for a position at the Port Angeles Plywood Mill. The work was hard, and they normally hired older people, but I managed to get a position. The plywood mill was located fifteen miles away on the other side of Port Angeles, near the water. The steam rose from the plywood kilns twenty-four hours a day. It was shift work—eight hours, twelve hours, or even sometimes a double shift of sixteen hours, which also meant getting paid time and a half. I joined the union of the International Woodworkers of America and got to know some interesting men and women, including former members of the sometimes controversial Industrial Workers of the World—the "Wobblies" as they were commonly known in earlier days of the labor movement.

There were different jobs: pushing the wet layers or sheets into the kilns that together made up a larger sheet of plywood, or working the receiving end, taking the finished plywood out of the kilns, now much heavier, and stacking it for further drying and sorting. My favorite assignment was working in the chip tower where I would shovel the wood chips used to fuel the steam-powered kilns. It was hard work but considered one of the more prestigious jobs at the mill, partly because it was hard manual labor. It paid 50 cents more per hour as well. The rich and poignant smell of burning wood and freshly cut wood chips permeated everything, including my clothes.

But I still had to contribute to room and board at home because my parents didn't make much money and struggled financially, and working at the mill did not cover my expenses and enable me to save for college. Unless I was working the all-night shift at the mill, I was expected to accompany Jefferson each night from just after midnight to 5:00 a.m. to clean the Dungeness Inn Golf Course Restaurant and Banquet Center. I would vacuum and then clean the toilets and the bathrooms on all three floors. Jefferson would clean the kitchen, including the hard work of cleaning the grease-caked commercial grills. Then he would mop the kitchen floors. If I finished before Jefferson, I would either play the piano downstairs in the banquet room or lie down on the banquet room carpet and take a nap. When Jefferson finished first, he would sometimes make us both a ham and cheese deli sandwich and pour a soda from the fountain machine before we would make our way back up the mountain to the log cabin. I generally slept in a couple of two-hour increments, between 10:00 p.m. and 12:00 a.m. and then again between 5:00 a.m. and 7:00 a.m.

The drive to the Dungeness Inn in Jefferson's precious green Dodge pickup truck, which by now was beginning to show signs of age, never seemed so hard because we would leave around midnight and I did better late at night. In fact, sometimes I was lucky to get home in time to leave with him. But the ride home at five in the morning was always harder for me. Most mornings on the way home, we didn't say much to each other. But there were mornings when a cougar would cross the road. Or we might see a deer. One morning, Jefferson told me he knew growing up like this wasn't always easy.

"Boy, I know it isn't easy being my number one son and having to work to help out the family," he said.

"I don't mind," I replied, "but sometimes I wish I could spend the same amount of time as others my age working on my own future."

"Jefferson, do you miss your grandkids?" I asked. "When I think of all the sacrifices you made, do you ever regret coming here so you and my mom could be together with me?"

"Boy, I never doubted that I'm supposed to be here and that you're supposed to be here."

He was proud of me and believed the Lord would bless me if I remembered that nothing was too great or too small to take on in this world. When we pulled up in front of the log cabin, the chickens were still asleep in the trees. Not even the poodle pack stirred. Somehow what Jefferson had said in just a few words made the early morning all right, put the daily trip to the Dungeness Inn in perspective, and made helping to support the family even better than okay.

In between working at the mill and the Dungeness Inn, I also took a course and studied for my real estate brokerage license. I wanted to have the option to sell local real estate. I thought deep down I could be a good salesman like Grandpa Whitey.

The highlight of the summer occurred when Whitey and Pauline, Ricky, and Patty came to visit. They had made it a tradition to visit every year in the late spring or summer. Sometimes they would stay for as long as a month. They would drive across country in their

Ricky and Patty

motor home, pulling a car or truck behind them, and Grandpa would sell the truck in Sequim to help pay for the trip. Grandpa Hughes was always ready to make a deal. I loved spending time with them. Besides my mom and Jefferson, Grandpa Hughes was my favorite person in the whole world. We would hook up an electrical cord from the cabin to the motor home. Then in the evenings around 8:00 p.m., when it was still light out on the Olympic Peninsula, Whitey and I would lie down in the motor home and read the latest *National Enquirer* tabloid article about how the aliens had been sighted or an article about the boy with the largest head in the world.

While Whitey and Pauline were visiting one summer, we drove the motor home west past Port Angeles to Neah Bay to go salmon fishing. Jerry, the boy from the detention center, was from Neah Bay. Coming here with Grandpa and Grandma made me think of Jerry and hope that he, too, had made his way in the world. Another weekend, the grandparents committed to taking me across by ferry to Seattle where I could sit for the real estate exam. That Friday, I had to work the night shift, so we left Sequim at 6:00 a.m. to catch the ferry. We barely made it in time for the 12:00 p.m. Saturday exam at a community college near Seattle. The exam lasted for several hours.

A week later the exam results arrived in the mail. I had failed by one point. I was so frustrated and disappointed; I knew I should have studied more. I thought, *if only I hadn't had to work all night the night before.* Why did this bad luck have to happen to me? Grandpa came upstairs to my door-less bedroom in the loft.

"Stop feeling sorry for yourself, Scottie. It just means you have to take it again. Never let your failures stand in the way and never blame anyone else. Remember to always focus on what you can do to make it right."

Grandpa helped me understand how important it was to not give up. I retook the exam and passed the second time. I even helped sell a piece of property and used the money for college.

After spending eight months working at the lumber mill, I finally arrived at the University of Puget Sound. During my time at the mill, I saved enough money to pay for one semester of college. Puget Sound was a prestigious small liberal arts school located in Tacoma, Washington. I was accepted for the fall semester. UPS was not as well known as Harvard, but it was often called the Harvard of the West. The campus was beautiful and what I imagined an Ivy League school would look like. Ivy covered the red brick buildings nestled under the Pacific Northwest canopy of the towering Douglas fir trees that surrounded the campus.

Jefferson was so proud of me and advised, "Boy just be yourself and know that you can make your own destiny."

If I couldn't land a scholarship or find a job, I'd have to drop out. My advisor, a professor in psychology, suggested that I only take one or two classes after reviewing my test scores. I explained that I only had funds for one semester and therefore needed to take a full course load. I chose history as a major and made all A's. After that, he always had a smile for me when I would see him on campus. Financially, I barely made it.

John Oppenheimer became one of my closest friends. We met in political science class on the first day of freshman year, and I remember seeing John surrounded by girls in the lecture hall. He came from a much different and well-to-do Jewish family, and he had the kind of personality you couldn't resist. When he was around, people gravitated toward him. John wasn't very tall, had lots of curls—which was the style at the time—and dressed real preppy, as if he could have been going to Harvard, which is where one of his brothers went. He wore a nice emerald green pullover sweater, white button-down shirt, and khaki pants complete with black loafers. In contrast, I wore jeans, a sweatshirt, and Frye boots, which I was proud of having recently purchased for college.

By spring of freshman year, John encouraged me to run for student body vice president. I thought he was crazy. It was not unlike high school, where one of the seniors convinced me to run. Oddly enough the slogan my college friends chose for me was "Action Jackson," just like in high school.

Student government helped pay for school. Eventually, so did many more scholarships and odd jobs. At the end of sophomore year, I ran for student body president. John signed on as my campaign adviser, and I won again. John volunteered as my co-director of public relations. As student body president, I served as the student representative to the university president's cabinet meetings and student representative to the university board of trustees. It was my job to translate. Sometimes I got it right and sometimes I didn't. I received the trust and respect from both students and the administration, because anyone could find me working day and night in the student union building.

Scott with fellow student body officers

I think if you work hard enough, even if you don't get it completely right, you earn the credibility to be heard. At UPS, I earned the credibility to be heard by all sides: students, faculty, administration, and even the trustees. There were major perks: My scholarship as a student body officer paid for room and board, and the president's executive assistant would even type my papers in a pinch.

The summer after junior year I was awarded a congressional internship in the office of US Senator Warren G. Magnuson. University of Puget Sound Board of Trustees Chair, Norton Clapp, supported my application for the internship. He also asked his stepson, Booth Gardner, to write a letter of support. Gardner would later be elected Washington State Governor. Another Congressman, Don Bonker, a Democrat representing the Third District, which included my hometown of Sequim, asked me to serve in his office, but Senator

Magnuson's acceptance arrived first. That summer I left Washington State for Washington, DC.

I spent as much time as possible visiting monuments and museums and getting to know the city. I attended Senate hearings and frequently visited the House and Senate floor galleries. I promised myself I would return as soon as I could.

Beyond the internship and learning about the US Capitol, a girl who I thought was the most beautiful girl in college said she was going to visit me and see the sights in Washington, DC, and she did. Together, we saw much of the city. We went to the Smithsonian American History Museum, and we rented a paddleboat at the Tidal Basin for spectacular views of the Jefferson and Lincoln memorials. We saw the US Capitol by moonlight and its outline in the reflecting pool below.

She even stayed with me in the basement apartment I was sharing for the summer, since my roommates were gone for most of her visit. We slept in different rooms; nothing ever happened physically between us. We came from different worlds. She was raised in a well-to-do middle class home in Minneapolis, but our friendship made me realize that someone like her might someday be interested in a poor kid from Sequim.

During the weekdays that summer, I would often work into the evenings and then walk home at dusk from the Dirksen Senate Office Building to my small summer apartment located not far from the Capitol near Union Station. I wandered through several transitional and poorer neighborhoods, and I would see the homeless finding their spots on the park benches or up against the corner of a building to rest for the night. One evening I decided to stay out there with them. I bought a cheap bottle of wine and a package of little cigars, the kind with the plastic cigarillo tips, and shared both with those I met. Sleeping on the park bench made me realize that none of us, regardless of circumstances, deserves to be neglected.

On Saturday mornings, I would linger at the local park and watch the pickup basketball games. Everyone who played was African

American. One Saturday I mustered the courage to ask if I could join them. After a pause and many disbelieving stares, there was a smile or two and I was added to a team. I wasn't very good, but I played all day and was one of the last ones to leave the basketball court.

Back at Puget Sound, I was reinvigorated. I didn't want college to end. I had grown to care about the people, and I knew they cared about me. Among the brick buildings and ivy vines, I felt safe and successful. I went on dates, had girlfriends, and on occasion I went to the fraternity and sorority parties. I would let down my guard and party with the best.

At the beginning of the school year, I was supposed to address the incoming freshmen during orientation week as their new student body president. Just before this, my good friend Scott, who had been elected with me as student body vice president—and who had recently returned from working on a fishing boat for the summer in Alaska—enticed me to come over to his dorm to do shots of tequila with all the beautiful freshman women. Scott was a resident assistant responsible for making sure the students in his dorm didn't get in trouble. I did the shots and then felt the effects as I walked with everyone to the stadium to give my remarks. I made it through my speech, but afterward I crawled my way into the stands to listen to the real president of the University and then blacked out.

The associate dean of students escorted me back to my room. The next morning, I called my friend Scott to let him know that someone had broken into my room and broken the toilet while I was sleeping naked on the couch, and several inches of water covered the floor. He rushed over, and we both realized all of what had happened was my own doing. It made me remember what my mom told me the night I left for college.

"Most kids who go to college waste their education. They party and never do anything important," she said. It was her way of trying to keep me headed in the right direction. I felt guilty enough to return to my studies.

With my closest college friends, I had shared my life story and how I got to the University of Puget Sound. My guy friends often wanted to come home with me during breaks to see the log cabin. One spring break, I brought four of my closest friends to Sequim. Whitey and Pauline were visiting, and Whitey served a delicious stew. He kept asking us if we liked it.

Yes, everyone liked it and had seconds and thirds. Then Whitey, with a smile on his face, told us we were eating horse meat he had brought from Missouri. I couldn't believe it. I was so embarrassed but my friends took it in good humor. They didn't have any more helpings, however. Jefferson got a big kick out of their reaction to Whitey and eating horsemeat. They were in awe of the cabin, but they were especially touched by meeting the Reverend Jefferson Jackson. They always wanted to spend more time with Jefferson and would even come with us to clean the Dungeness Inn and eat deli sandwiches.

By the time graduation arrived, it seemed a lifetime had passed since my days in Kansas. I woke up early on that Saturday. Jefferson was taking a rare day off work from the golf course (at least one of his jobs), and he and Mom were driving over that morning. Their arrival wasn't just important for me; Jefferson had been selected to deliver the baccalaureate sermon at Kilworth Chapel.

The service was set to begin at 11:30 a.m. By 10:30, they still hadn't arrived, and I began to worry. Two hours of one-lane highway separated Sequim from Tacoma. This was only their second time visiting campus; their first was when I arrived as a freshman. As my panic increased, they pulled up. They gave me a pendant to wear on my robe that said "the world's greatest son" and a graduation card with lines from the poem *Desiderata* by Max Ehrmann. The words of the poem had meaning to me:

You are a child of the universe, no less than the trees and the stars;
you have a right to be here.
And whether or not it is clear to you, no doubt the
universe is unfolding as it should.

We rushed to Kilworth Chapel on the other side of campus. Inside the red brick building, we made our way to the front. Jefferson and I took our places near the pulpit. By the time the service started, hundreds of people crowded the pews behind Mom. Looking out, I saw John and Deanna, his girlfriend and later wife, and remembered that first day of class when we met. It seemed like yesterday and a lifetime ago at the same time.

I introduced Jefferson to the crowd. As always, he preached without notes. Even though he never finished high school, his eloquence captured the crowd with ease, truth, and passion. When he spoke to a nearly all-white audience about God, and how important it was to "love thy neighbor," people listened closely to this man's message of love and forgiveness.

After the service we proceeded to the main ceremony. I had missed my high school graduation by leaving early for New Zealand, so this ceremony assumed even more importance. University President Philip Phibbs and his wife Gwen had become my mentors and family away from home. I even lived one summer with another close college friend, Jeff Koontz, in the basement of the president's residence and served dinner to the governor of the state of Washington, among others, as part of my assigned duties. Still, I was shocked when President Phibbs addressed me directly during his speech:

Scott has distinguished himself in scholarship and leadership of the
student body. Scott has been a partner to me and to the university in
every way. Most significantly, there's no other student that I believe
has made more of a difference to the university during my tenure as
president than Scott Jackson.

Scott receiving his diploma from President Phil Phibbs

I was overwhelmed. I looked for Mom and Jefferson in the crowd, and I thought about what we'd been through. I thought about the night I ran away from Dad. I remembered the abuse, and again I wondered what could have been, even more than what this mission had become. In leaving Dad, I chose Mom and Jefferson. But I also chose a childhood of paucity over a middle-class income and lifestyle. In running toward unconditional love, I unwittingly also ran toward economic hardship I never considered. Despite all that, I graduated with many honors. Still, I couldn't help but wonder if my achievements could have been greater had I not been forced to choose.

Imagining what life would have been like with Dad—or if my mom and dad hadn't broken up—was hard sometimes. It was in these moments I could imagine a happy family, playing basketball on the varsity team, and even having girlfriends who didn't run away after learning about my family. I imagined attending an Ivy League school. But then I wouldn't be Scott Jackson, Jefferson's number one son. I would be someone else and I wouldn't have had Jefferson in my life. I knew I was where I was meant to be.

As graduation day drew to a close, Mom and Jefferson drove back to Sequim. Jefferson had to be at work by four o'clock the next morning. His "number one son" might have experienced one of the biggest days of his life, but the Dungeness Inn still needed to be cleaned.

Before he left for Sequim, Jefferson reached over and gave me a big hug, smiled, and said, "Boy, I am mighty proud of you. Know what they will remember about you is that your heart is the biggest they have seen."

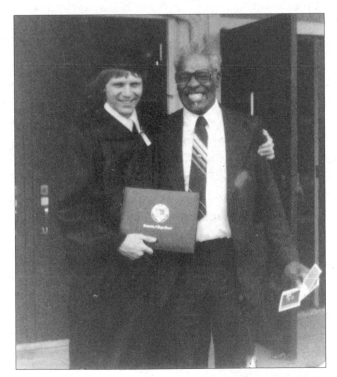

Scott and Jefferson at graduation

Pursuing Education: The Great Equalizer

More than one trillion dollars is spent on education, and yet black students have only a 69 percent high school graduation rate, and Hispanic students have a 73 percent rate, in contrast with an 88 percent rate for Asians and an 86 percent rate for Caucasians. Thirty years ago the United States was ranked number 1 for the amount of people receiving secondary education diplomas. Today, the US is ranked 30th in the world for their high school graduation rate.

De Tocqueville in his observing of American culture wrote: "It cannot be doubted that, in the United States, the instruction of the people powerfully contributes to the support of a democratic republic." Yet, today 1.3 million US secondary students don't graduate on time. Fifty percent of those who attend college will take six years or more to get their undergraduate degree.

Worldwide there are 57 million school-aged children who are not in school. Girls represent more than half of those not in school. Two thirds of illiterate people in the world are women. In Sub-Saharan Africa, 11.7 million children leave school before completing primary education.

Of those fortunate enough to attend secondary school, it is estimated that for every year of secondary school completed, a child's future earning potential increases as much as 25 percent. Access to safe schools, trained teachers, adequate school supplies, and tuition fees is a proven and essential formula for breaking the cycle of poverty. Children born to educated mothers are less likely to be stunted or malnourished, increasing their odds of having healthy and productive lives.

Like many young people in the United States and around the world, it wasn't easy for me to complete my education. It was easier than it was for Jefferson, my black stepfather, who was given his first pair of shoes by his teacher, to walk several miles to school and back before working on the family farm. But it was also not easy for me at times.

Because my father beat my mother during my elementary school years, I would shut the door and play war with toy soldiers and dominoes instead of doing my homework. In middle school my school work was interrupted when my mom and I frequently ran away from my father and hid out on a horse ranch in the Olympic Mountains. When I did finally catch up in school, I was taken away from my home and returned to my father in Kansas, where I ran away again.

During high school I worked a full-time job as a box boy for the Southwoods dry goods store because my family didn't have enough money to attend an elite private college or university without a substantial scholarship. I had to work hard to earn enough money in order to begin a semester in college and hope that I would have enough funds to remain. Even in college, I came home during every break and worked in the Plywood Mill.

*Scott with his mother at the University of Puget Sound when
he received his honorary PhD in Letters in 2010*

But when it was just me studying in the University of Puget Sound Collins Library, alone with the philosopher Reinhold Niebuhr or enveloped in the study of the Civil Rights Movement, I learned that the great equalizer is education and knowledge. No socioeconomic class can take away what you learn. Even more important is what you can do in the world with such knowledge. For today's young men and women alike, we can't afford not to invest in their education. The cost of not investing is simply too great. Everyone deserves a decent education, and it's important for the advancement of our entire world that we make significant strides in education globally and work diligently to reduce the number of children who do not receive even a primary school education.

GLOBAL GOAL 4

Quality Education

Ensure inclusive and equitable quality education and promote lifelong learning opportunities for all

During the conflict in the Syrian Arab Republic, ordinary choices about whether to send a child to school or to a playground have become tragic life-and-death decisions. As of 2016, one quarter of all schools no longer functioned because they are either damaged, destroyed, or used as shelters to host families fleeing violence. Syria's education sector has lost more than 52,000 teachers. More than two million Syrian children have been forced to drop out of school because of displacement caused by the fighting, destruction or closure of schools, and lack of teachers. The conflict has also forced children out of school in other ways—when their parents are killed by fighting, when they are separated from family members, when they are forced into work to support their families, and when girls are forced into early marriages, often by parents who hope this will help keep them safer from violence.

Charities in Action

UNITED STATES FUND

UNICEF is committed to ensuring that all children—regardless of gender, ethnicity, socioeconomic background, or circumstances—realize their right to a quality education.

Save the Children believes every child deserves a future. In the U.S. and around the world, we ensure children have the opportunity to learn and develop the skills they need to succeed. We do whatever it takes for children—every day and in times of crisis—transforming their lives and the future we share.

Children International is a leader in the movement to eradicate poverty. From toddler to young adulthood, we surround kids with a caring team, a safe place and a clear path out of poverty through programs focused on health, education, empowerment and employment.

CHAPTER NINE

Following My Dream

For all the closure college graduation seemed to bring, it carried with it just as many questions. Mom invited me to spend the summer back home, "helping Jefferson clean the Inn." Nothing could have put the fear of God in me more.

I'd been named an alternate for the post-graduate Rotary Foundation Ambassadorial Scholarship program, but it would be months before I knew if I'd travel overseas. Even if I did receive a placement, it would be a year before I actually departed.

Ideally, I wanted a job in Washington, DC. But without money, nights at the Dungeness Inn looked more and more likely. I applied for jobs at every egalitarian organization or government group in Tacoma. They all rejected me. I couldn't believe it: I was one of the most successful students in recent UPS history, and I was about to begin my post-college career unemployed.

Desperate for a solution, I organized a painting crew, together with my close friend Scott, and lined up more than a dozen jobs, mostly for faculty and staff at UPS. I rented a house near campus and spent that summer putting my newly minted degree to work painting houses.

Summer passed quickly. Each house presented its own challenges, but we never fell behind schedule. I bought an old Mini, whose brakes failed in the very first week, and traded it in for a small Datsun pickup truck. Besides, I reasoned, I could move my stuff to DC with a truck and sleep in back along the way.

All summer I thought about the plan John and I had put together near the end of school. He'd landed a job in DC and intended to rent a place with a second bedroom. John worked for a former member of Congress who had founded a small research institute that engaged members of Congress with corporations and other constituencies in their districts at conferences and through newsletters. The congressman also happened to own the townhouse in which John and I would be living. I just needed to get there by fall. And find a job in DC while working on the other side of the country. I was so set on DC that I even turned down a job as a UPS admissions counselor.

I had second thoughts, but I knew my dream.

As summer neared its end and I was painting my next-to-last house with my crew, Congressman Don Bonker called me. His district included Sequim. Even though I had chosen Senator Magnuson's office over his for my internship, Bonker still remembered me. Unfortunately, the congressman wasn't calling to ask me to DC. Instead, he wanted me on his Washington State campaign team in Olympia. I accepted a one-month volunteer position as his driver and reported for duty as the new paint on the last house dried. My first day on the job nearly ruined my career.

When I arrived in the campaign office for the first time, some of the staff seemed surprised to see me. The woman who ran the office welcomed me and began to introduce me as the congressman's new driver. A few minutes later, the door flung open and a young woman with dark curly hair bounced past. Her name was Gretchen, and she was in charge of the congressman's schedule.

"The congressman's already late," she said. "Here are the keys. The car is out front. Here are your directions. You're going to the Nisqually Delta."

She explained how the congressman was scheduled to accept an award for a housing grant he supported for a local American Indian tribe. A rival Democrat was also expected to be there.

"But this is Congressman Bonker's award," Gretchen said sternly. "So get him there first."

"Got it," I said. "Just two questions. Where's the congressman? And where is the Nisqually Delta?"

Right then Don Bonker walked through the door.

"Scott 'Action' Jackson. Good to see you. You made it."

That's all it took to get my blood flowing. Just like that, I was at the heart of a congressional campaign.

The congressman and I made our way outside and into the campaign car, a large LTD Ford that used to be his dad's. As we pulled away, I tried to forget how awful I was at navigating while driving. In fact, I wasn't even that great at driving.

The congressman directed me to the highway and north toward the Nisqually Delta. After we got off the highway, he seemed a bit lost.

"Go right! No, left!" he said.

His frustration came on suddenly and made me nervous. When I looked at the controls in front of me, I really became scared. For the first time since leaving the office, I realized we were low on gas. In fact, the needle was on empty. After a few more minutes of driving around lost, the car sputtered. When it jerked to a stop somewhere near the middle of the Nisqually Delta, I panicked.

At first, the congressman handled it well. When we turned on the radio, we both realized the severity of our situation. The local news was covering a story about a congressman receiving great accolades. It was Don Bonker's rival, accepting his award.

Fortunately, my days on the campaign trail improved. The congressman seemed to like having me around, and I was learning a lot about campaigns. I also met a bunch of interesting people, like George the sign man who drove a beat-up station wagon, with the back full of Bonker signs and a poodle in the passenger seat. The congressman was big on signs, and the sign man canvassed the district to deliver them to everyone in the third district who wanted one.

During my month on the campaign, I sometimes ran errands without the congressman. Once, he sent me to Sequim at the same time George was delivering signs in the area, so I invited George to the log cabin for dinner.

It was after dark before George found his way down the gravel driveway through the fir trees to the house Mom and Jefferson had built. I was always anxious when people arrived for the first time. Most of the friends I had brought during college saw the cabin as a fairy tale-like home in the woods. Its high ceilings and uneven floors held a quaint nursery rhyme quality they had never seen before. A few visitors, however, took one look at the place and couldn't believe anyone lived inside.

Since George had his own set of unusual qualities, I didn't think he'd be too surprised. Boy was I wrong. As the sign man walked to the front door carrying his poodle, I could see the shock register on his face. Inside, Moe the South American Macaw, with a wingspan of more than four feet, greeted him with a guttural cry while Super Cat, Mom's twenty-pound ball of fur and claws, attempted to draw blood. Also shocking to George was the pack of miniature poodle mixes that charged and began yapping around his feet. The pack represented what was left of three generations of litters—the descendants of Trixie—that Mom had chosen not to sell and now let rule the house. George clutched his own poodle protectively as Mom attempted to herd the dogs away.

The poodle pack had developed quite the lore around our house, mostly because of the incident with the rooster. Big Red was the biggest and meanest rooster we had ever raised. Jeffie-Lou and Shawne were both scared of him and would huddle together whenever he got close. Big Red was so large that we once hooked him up to a cart and let him pull it along the entire parade route during the Irrigation Festival. So confident had Big Red become in his dominance that he began to terrorize the poodle pack—that is, until the incident.

I forget who found Big Red hiding, but it quickly became clear that the poodle pack had somehow organized an attack. By the time we found him, Big Red was missing most of his feathers. He was never quite so mean again. The poodle pack, however, gained so much confidence that it started acting more like a pack of wolves than anything domesticated. All this all happened not long before George showed up for dinner.

Unfortunately, George never ate dinner that night. Just as Mom cleared her poodle pack from the living room, Jeffie-Lou poked her head through the second-floor balcony rails. Jefferson was in the kitchen, cooking something in a large pot.

"Cottie, you're just in time," she yelled out. "Daddy killed a raccoon and he's cooking it up for supper."

George's face went pale. He rushed out the door and back to his station wagon, empty of all the Bonker signs he'd delivered earlier that day. As he drove away, the poodle pack barked behind him.

As my month on the campaign trail came to an end, I told the congressman I was leaving for Washington, DC. What little savings I had was running out. I knew if I didn't go soon, I might never leave at all. A permanent future with the poodle pack and Big Red seemed far more likely than I wanted to consider. The congressman stopped short of offering me a job, but said he looked forward to seeing me back east. We shook hands and I left the congressman's campaign office for the last time.

A few days later, I packed up my red pickup truck, complete with camper top, and hit the road. Outside Ashland, Oregon, I pulled over for my first night on the road and climbed into the back of the truck. As I fell asleep, I wondered if I had made the right decision. I had nothing promised and everything invested in finding a job in DC.

As I made my way across country, the Democrats lost many seats that first Tuesday night in November 1980. However, Congressman Bonker had won easily. For me, it was the only highlight of a night that also saw Ronald Reagan, the actor and former conservative governor of California, beat incumbent Jimmy Carter and become the 40th President of the United States. The election results also meant there would be fewer options for young Democrats in DC. After four full days of driving, with short nights spent at truck stops, I was within striking distance of the capital.

I entered the beltway approaching the nation's capital with the evening rush hour. Nearly two hours later, I parked in front of a townhouse on East Capitol Street, just two blocks from the US Supreme Court. John was inside hosting a farewell party for congressional staffers who worked for US Senator Frank Church from Idaho, a former Democratic presidential candidate. They had all lost their jobs in the wake of the Reagan Republican landslide. It had been one of the worst election nights ever for Democrats.

After the farewell party ended, John and I sat alone in the living room, eating leftover crackers and cheese. Just as he said he would, John had saved me a bedroom on the third floor of the townhouse. That night, my mind raced with anticipation. I barely slept. Almost two years since my internship in Senator Magnuson's office, I had finally arrived back in the nation's capital. Now there was one last hurdle: finding a job.

The next day, John and I planned to meet for lunch. Walking along the Mall, I once again felt awestruck by the grandeur of the buildings and monuments that stand at the center of American government and history. I arrived at Congressman Bonker's office a few minutes before 9:00 a.m. when the office officially opened. A Washington State flag hung near the door. I entered a small reception area, and a beautiful woman with blonde hair welcomed me.

"Do you have an appointment?" she asked in a British accent that startled me.

Scott Jackson and his friend John Oppenheimer

"No," I replied. "But I just worked on the campaign with the congressman, and he told me to come see him when I arrived in DC. I'm hoping he can squeeze me in."

Another voice responded from behind me. "Congressman Bonker is in the office today, but he has a very busy schedule and a number of visits ahead of him," a woman said. "I'll see what I can do."

It was the congressman's executive assistant. She had just left the congressman's office, closed the door behind her, and invited me to wait. An hour later, Don Bonker walked out.

"Scott Jackson, you made it." The congressman sounded pleased to see me, but his tone changed quickly. We walked from his office to the House floor. Inside the US Capitol, frescos swarmed above us. Small desks filled the room, and the podium where the president delivers the State of the Union Address stood at the front. I knew I needed to be a part of this.

"This is the worst time for Democrats in thirty years," Bonker said. "I don't have a spot open in my office, and former staffers from other offices are lining up for work, even if I could make room for someone."

I knew election night hadn't gone well, but I didn't realize how widespread the ramifications would be. The congressman left me at the entrance to the House floor and told me to return to his office after lunch.

In the meantime, I knew I needed a backup plan. I found my way to the office of Norm Dicks, the congressional representative who had beat us that day we ran out of gas on the Nisqually Delta. A couple of years earlier, I had hosted Dicks as student body president during a visit he made to the UPS campus. When I arrived at his office, his chief of staff took a meeting with me.

"Times are tough, Scott," he said, echoing Bonker. "We don't have anything right now, but let me think about it."

I walked outside and across the Capitol grounds. The office of Senator Magnuson was full of boxes. Staffers were packing their desks. Very few had any idea where their next job would be. I left before anyone could tell me again that it was the worst time for Democrats in thirty years.

John and I met for lunch at a place called Bull Feathers, named after President Teddy Roosevelt, located on Capitol Hill, not far from Congressman Bonker's office. At lunch, I looked at John in disbelief. Less than a day into my job hunt, it had become clear that my chances were bleak.

John listened carefully.

"How'd you leave it with Congressman Bonker's office?" he asked.

"I'm going back there after lunch to continue our discussion," I replied.

"Well, that's good," John said. "Now all you have to do is be yourself."

Before we left, I asked the waitress for an application.

When I returned to Congressman Bonker's office, his executive assistant told me he was in meetings for the next few hours. I waited in the entry area until four o'clock. When he reappeared, he was in a hurry to get to a hearing. Again, we walked and talked. We made our way down the hall to the elevator. As we did, the congressman talked about staffing commitments that were already made.

"There's really nothing we can do right now," he said.

The elevator doors closed behind us, leaving us alone for the first time all day. I felt my one and only opportunity slipping away.

"Congressman," I said, somewhat loudly, causing him to look right at me. "I will work twenty-four hours a day, seven days a week, for nothing. Just put me on staff." I learned this from Jefferson.

He seemed surprised. My plea had caught him off guard.

"For nothing," he said. "You have to eat."

"Pay me what you can. I'll get a second job. Put me on staff and I'll do whatever it takes. There's nothing too big or too small."

The elevator doors opened and we walked in silence. When we arrived at the hearing, Bonker looked me right in the eye. "We'll talk after the hearing."

I sat in the audience and waited. When the hearing ended, we walked together back to his office. Along the way, he talked about the kind of work I would be doing if I joined the office. I could help with legislative correspondence, prepare meeting notes, help him get places on time, and do anything else other office staffers needed.

"It won't be glamorous," he said.

"It sounds perfect," I said.

At the office, I again waited in the entry area while the congressman spoke with his office manager. When she came out, she officially offered me the job.

"You're hired," she said. "We can pay you seven hundred dollars a month. Your job is yet undefined, but the congressman wants you on staff."

I could hardly believe it.

The congressman came out a few minutes later.

"I can't thank you enough," I said.

"We start at nine o'clock," he replied. "See you in the morning."

The next few months flashed by. I wore a tie every morning and always arrived early. I sat at a small desk near the congressman's office. No two days were the same; order and predictability took a back seat

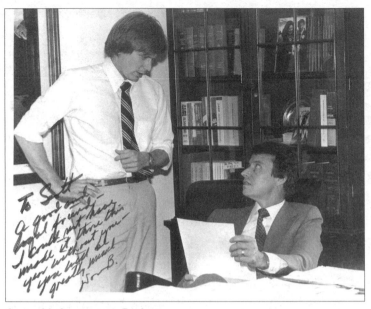

Scott with Congressman Bonker

to the issues of the day. I strived to respond with calm and helped however I could. One minute, I'd meet with constituents visiting from back home. The next, I'd drive the congressman across town. I learned the city quickly and always made sure there was gas in the car. I also helped keep track of his work with small businesses, the Department of Veterans Affairs, international trade, and humanitarian issues.

At Bullfeather's, where I had submitted my application that first day when John and I had met for lunch, I was the only English-speaking busboy at the time. I also helped the congressman with odd jobs around his house.

I fell in love with Washington, even more than when I had been there as an intern. John and I made many friends and hosted parties. We went to lunch on the weekends when I wasn't working, read *The Washington Post*, watched Sunday morning political commentators, and visited the Senate gallery during midnight filibusters. Washington quickly became my home. But almost as soon as I grew comfortable, the past came back into focus.

It was springtime when Dad called. I recognized his voice immediately. The last time we had seen each other was still that final day outside the courtroom in Port Angeles. I recalled watching him choke Mom and the day I ran away for good. Talking to him brought back memories I wanted to bury. It also made me wonder once again how my life could have been different, if only he had lived up to the words he used to preach. As our conversation wore on, my anger grew. I felt robbed of a childhood and opportunity. Whatever success I achieved came despite my family and financial challenges. The moral and spiritual support provided by Sydney and Jefferson had helped immensely, but it could never completely fill the void.

Dad and I had spoken only a few times in the past nine years. My mom had written a letter to my grandmother on my dad's side letting her know I was an exchange student in New Zealand. As a result, my grandmother had written to me to try to re-establish sporadic contact between Dad and me.

In her letters Grandma Agnes would tell me how proud she was of me and then she would recount the details of their whereabouts and whatever was happening at church. She would almost invariably end with a sentence or two, or more, about Dad—how he missed me, how he needed me, and how he wanted to write himself, but that I should write him first. It was never about how he was sorry and how he wanted to support me—financially or otherwise. The guilt and the anger inside me would collide with the perseverance and the independence in my life and jumble it all together. Ultimately, I would need to find balance. The kind of balance Jefferson portrayed every day just to walk down the street.

During our phone call, Dad mentioned that he and his second wife were coming to DC for a church conference, where he would also preach that Sunday at the National City Christian Church located on Thomas Circle.

"We'd like to spend some time with you," he said.

I didn't know what to say. It had been a long time since I had even thought about my dad. I hadn't yet forgiven him for anything that happened and wasn't sure I ever could.

"Let's play it by ear," I said, maybe because I didn't know how to say no.

As I hung up the phone, I knew I couldn't get out of it. I told John what had happened, and he offered to go to dinner with us. I was relieved. At least I wouldn't have to face Dad alone.

A couple of weeks later, Dad and his wife arrived at our townhouse by taxi. As they walked up the sidewalk, I had a visceral feeling about this. He looked as stern and disapproving as he had when he was bringing me back to Kansas. It wasn't fair. What I saw in him was everything I didn't want to be. The way he looked. How much he weighed. His mannerisms. Everything I saw made me angry.

I did my best to calm down and answer the door. We sat in the living room with John and talked for a while.

Dad grimaced as he sat down. He started to tell John why they were here and explained that he would be preaching on Sunday at the National City Christian Church. John asked more about his work with the church. The entire time all I could do was think about how unfair it was to be sitting in this living room, pretending that he was part of my life. Fortunately for me, John carried the conversation. More fortunate for me, we finally left for dinner.

We went to a restaurant in downtown Washington, DC, Charlie's Crab House, not far from the White House and the National Mall. We mostly made small talk. They never asked about Mom or Jefferson, and they asked only a little about me. I had been accepted as a Rotary International Ambassadorial Scholar a few weeks earlier and told them as much. Dad offered to help with my overseas expenses but never followed through. I don't think I really expected him to.

After dinner we walked in front of the White House. They caught a cab back to their hotel, and John and I walked home.

John then casually said, "That wasn't so bad. They seemed nice enough."

I lashed out at my beloved friend. "Are you kidding?" I said. "How does he come here and pretend everything is okay or that there is nothing to ask forgiveness for?"

My balance was a work in progress.

After Dad's visit, I committed myself to work even harder and began to prepare for my year overseas. My acceptance as a Rotary scholar would send me to the University of Edinburgh in Scotland for an MBA. Things were finally falling into place. The cherry blossoms lined my morning jog along the National Mall, and I found myself feeling a bit nostalgic about leaving this place I had come to love. I wanted a degree that would stick and that would work around the world, and one that I could get in less than two years—and I had to have a scholarship. I didn't want to do something that wasn't well-known or practical. The thirteenth-month program at Edinburgh fit all my requirements.

As spring turned into summer, I began to organize fundraising events for the congressman. Other Democratic members of congress began to notice me. Life was good. One day around this time, the congressman invited me into his office and asked me to close the door. I wasn't sure what to expect.

"Scott," he said. "I have the perfect girl for you."

I was shocked. I rarely talked about my dating life. Apparently, the congressman had taken more of an interest in my personal life than I knew.

I had very few dates in high school. On the rare occasions when a girl took an interest in me or vice versa, my mom or I would invariably receive a call from the girl's parents. They would let us know that while I was respected in school and in the Sequim Community, they could not take the chance that their daughter would become seriously involved with and part of an interracial family. The call would usually end with the parents explaining that they hoped we would understand; it was nothing personal. It was easier in New Zealand than in college. But I always knew that as soon as someone learned more about what I had been through as a child, and about my family and the color of Jefferson's skin, there could be deeply rooted prejudice and concerns for appearances that could not always be overcome.

There was another reason why I didn't date or, for that matter, have many close friends. Deep down I didn't believe I was worthy. It was easier for me to focus on others than allow the focus to be on me. By doing so, I could keep from having to share my story and wouldn't have to confront my own fears. After all, I still fought the anger inside me. My father had been abusive and his father before him. Yes, I had Jefferson and Sydney as role models to help break the cycle, and yet I knew that I constantly had to choose the positive and not allow the anger to overtake me. Keeping to myself, I could keep others from hurting me, too.

The congressman began to tell me about Dana. She worked for The Fellowship and helped organize the National Prayer Breakfast. She had recently graduated from Sweet Briar College and was earning extra money babysitting for the congressman. He thought we would make a great pair. Apparently, we both attended National Presbyterian Church but had never met.

A few weeks after the congressman told me about her, he brought Dana on staff as his new executive assistant. She had less experience than I had when he had taken a chance on hiring me. Our desks were only a few feet apart, and I couldn't stop watching her work. She had chestnut hair, green eyes, a beautiful smile, and a way with people. She was kind, gentle, and accepting of me. Our first date soon followed. From that night on, we became friends and were together more often than not. Little did I know then that someday she would become my fiancée.

I spent most of the summer with Dana, and suddenly it was fall, and I had to leave for graduate school. When I arrived in Edinburgh, the cold Scottish wind welcomed me as if to acknowledge that everything I had heard about Scottish weather was indeed true. The day was cold and gray. It was September, and school, located in the heart of historic Edinburgh, would soon begin.

On the first day of class, I walked across a campus full of history and checked in with the business school. Each of my forty-member student cohorts had an assigned desk and locker. Every professor had his or her own office, and there was one lecture hall with smaller classrooms across the corridor from the professors.

I made my way to upper campus and onto the cobblestones of High Street. At the bottom of High Street stood the queen's residence. At the top, Edinburgh Castle. The postgraduate dormitory was a centuries old stone structure constructed originally to serve the castle. My room came complete with two roommates and a radiator that produced only eight hours of heat per a twenty-four-hour period.

The classes at the University of Edinburgh were the hardest I'd ever taken: statistics, microeconomics, macroeconomics, and marketing theory. Weekdays included six hours of class and a late lunch followed by six hours of studying and homework. I had only a few friends, including Kaka, a Nigerian who was nothing short of a genius when it came to numbers. Kaka was quiet and kept to himself by habit and also because of his "different-ness." He lived in the same dorm as I did on High Street next to the castle. After class, we would find ourselves walking back to the dorm together. I was one of the only classmates to reach out to Kaka. We started having lunch together on the way home, stopping at the student union building for a curry.

Just before the end of the first week of class, I received a call at the dormitory. A Scottish gentleman named Alex Wilkie was on the other end of the line. Alex owned a women's clothing store in town and would serve as my Rotary host father during my time in Edinburgh.

"I'll pick you up for Rotary tomorrow and then we can go to the club for a whiskey," he said, not asking any questions.

Alex and his family became my support group in Scotland. I told them all about my family and my hope that I would soon get married. We attended church together, enjoyed Sunday night dinners, and shared whiskey with haggis. Alex Wilkie reminded me of a Scottish well-to-do Whitey Hughes. He was confident yet kind. He enjoyed life but was generous to a fault. I never could enjoy the taste of Haggis, but the Wilkies were like family.

During this time, I also managed to continue my commitment to exercise, running four to six miles on most days. Scottish weather proved challenging, and strong winds followed by sheets of diagonal rain became part of my regular routine. So did short winter days and long damp nights.

The brutal exam system at Edinburgh also came as a jolt. Each student's ability to analyze a subject and make cognitive arguments about conclusions was judged without reserve. Worse for me, bad handwriting wasn't tolerated. My scores were so low after my first midterms that I risked not passing half my classes. I met with the professors, took their advice, and rededicated myself to studying even harder.

When Christmas arrived, I boarded a plane back to the East Coast, according to plan. Dana was waiting for me at the airport. We spent a few days at her parents' home in Maryland, just outside Washington, DC. From there, we flew to Denver for an unexpected side trip to visit my brother Shawne at National Jewish Hospital, where he was being treated for severe asthma. Shawne was now fifteen and his condition had worsened over the years. National Jewish Hospital accepted him as a patient without cost in the hope that they could stabilize his condition and improve treatment. Mom and Jefferson were also there, along with Jeffie-Lou. Shawne was glad to see us.

In Denver, heavy snow began to fall. A blizzard enveloped the city. Huge blankets of snow covered the ground, and the wind chill dropped temperatures to thirty degrees below zero. It reminded me of the night I ran away, and I was grateful to be warm and cozy inside. The airport closed. It remained that way through Christmas Eve. We kept our hotel rooms where Jefferson and Sydney were also stranded, and waited out the storm. The blizzard kept the airport shut for thirty-three hours. Dana and I ate Christmas Eve dinner in the hotel restaurant while Jefferson, Sydney, and Jeffie-Lou ordered room service.

We finally left late on Christmas Day and returned to Maryland. My time was running out. Two days after Christmas, I asked Dana's dad for her hand. Later that night, I proposed. I offered her the same wedding ring Grandma Hughes once wore. It was small, with a few diamonds around a blue sapphire. She said yes. I returned to Edinburgh before the New Year.

Throughout our time in Sequim, couples would seek out Jefferson for marriage counseling and to officiate at their weddings. Some were first marriages and others were second marriages or beyond. Either way, Jefferson's counsel was always consistent yet focused: "Be yourself, always put the other person first, believe in each other, and put your faith in God and always in a higher person. Forbear and forgive each other regardless of the circumstances. Love each other always."

We set the date for our wedding, and I returned to Edinburgh and to my daily regimen of school and studies. June arrived and my exams came in quick succession, three hours each, two a day, for three days. If I passed, I'd then be able to return after the wedding to complete a final dissertation and receive my MBA. When the exams came to an end, I had hardly a moment to relax.

The next morning I boarded a plane back to the states. My wedding day was less than a week away.

The reception took place at Kenwood Country Club, which until the late 1970s didn't allow black members or guests. John Oppenheimer agreed to be my best man. He also made the townhouse available for a bachelor party and for my side of the wedding party to stay while in Washington, DC. Mom, Jefferson, and Jeffie-Lou arrived the week before the wedding. Grandpa and Grandma Hughes also came, as well as a few family friends from Sequim. Shawne was still in Denver at the hospital and couldn't make it.

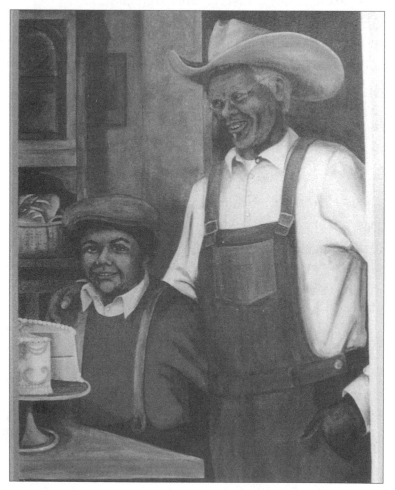

Sequim mural of Jefferson and Shawne

The entire week Whitey was always the first person up at the townhouse.

One morning, John Oppenheimer asked him, "Whitey why are you always up so early?"

Whitey replied, "I read somewhere most people die in their sleep and I want to beat the odds."

A few months earlier, I had told Dad he wasn't invited. I had been receiving letters regularly since his visit to DC. He often asked about our wedding plans, and I avoided responding for a while. When I finally did, he took the news harshly. Perhaps it was this decision that prevented him from making good on his previous promise to support me financially with my studies in Edinburgh.

I knew my decision would impact our relationship for a long time. But it wasn't about revenge or anything like that. As far as I was concerned, Dad lost the right to be my father when he began to abuse my mom, and even more so when he tried to take me away from her. In some way, I suppose he lost the right the first time he hit Mom when she was pregnant. I didn't want him at my wedding, and I didn't want to pretend he was something he wasn't. I believe Dad realized his role in our failed father-son relationship. He forced me to choose. He forced me away from the life into which I had been born. I now saw Jefferson as my father, and to invite my biological father felt like a betrayal of my mom and Jefferson.

As far as I was concerned, my only hope at a normal life was to separate myself from that history as clearly as possible. I had experienced enough emotional bruises already. My wedding day wasn't a place for more.

The ceremony took place in National Presbyterian Church, a grand building with a massive sanctuary. A pipe organ and floor-to-ceiling stained-glass windows filled the cavernous hall. More than three hundred people attended our ceremony. Dana looked beautiful as she walked down the aisle. She was more than I ever imagined I deserved. I realized I might not have been seen as the ideal candidate for a husband. After all, I was a poor kid from Sequim with an inter-racial family. We were two young people who had persevered to make our way in our respective journeys. We shared a commitment to do something good for others in the world. Jefferson stood at the front of the church with fellow pastor Louis Evans.

The day after the wedding, we flew to London and on to Edin-burgh. We arrived just in time for the posting of final exam scores. Students gathered in tight clusters as administrators hung lists of names and scores. Mine came in well above average, which meant I passed and could proceed with my thesis.

Over the next few months, I completed my MBA. The following school year I finished a dissertation that focused on international trade. Afterward we traveled across Scotland, England, Germany, France, and Switzerland before returning to the states aboard the Queen Elizabeth II, the most famous cruise ship in the world at the time.

Understanding the Politics of of Global Development

The United States spends $35 billion in foreign assistance, supporting the military and non-military development aid of the rest of the world. Most Americans think this is a much larger part of our federal budget and tax-payers' money than it really is. In reality, we spend less than .02 percent of our annual budget on aid. Most developed countries spend much closer to the global target of .07 percent of their budget on foreign aid. Furthermore, a large proportion of what we do spend is allocated to countries considered strategic allies of the United States, rather than countries on the basis of need.

Of our $35 billion in foreign assistance, almost a quarter of those funds aid the following five countries: Israel $3.1 billion, Egypt $1.5 billion, Afghanistan $1.1 billion, Jordan $ 1.0 billion, and Pakistan $ 933 million. By geographic region, Africa receives 20 percent, the Middle East 20 percent, South and Central Asia 7 percent, the Western Hemisphere that includes Central and Latin America, 4 percent.

Approximately 76 percent of the world received some form of economic assistance from the US. These numbers do not include support from multilateral aid agencies, corporations, or the private sector, including individual donors, foundations, and corporations, which account for another $ 5.1 billion annually.

More than half of the world's poor live in less developed countries, while significantly less than half of foreign aid reaches the less developed countries. Despite the size of these numbers, poor countries draw the short straw in terms of foreign assistance from public and private donors, according to new data by the Organization for Economic Cooperation and Development (OECD). Global official development assistance grew to $137.2 billion in 2014, an all-time high, but the money going to the least developed countries (LDCs) actually was less than previous years. Increasing numbers of refugees (such as those from Sudan and Syria) means that the gap is widening. Money going to the least developed countries (LDCs) has fallen by $2 billion, and LDCs' overall share was at a decade low. Funding for the Global Goals is estimated to be short by as much as $1 trillion dollars per year. This is also not good news.

It is important to acknowledge that once the aid does arrive, it is not always used effectively and, hopefully even less often, there is a misuse of funds. The Global Development community must use the Global Goals framework to make progress on these issues and to effectively measure against established targets. But we can't hold these funds accountable for achieving the Global Goals unless they are allocated to the countries and people in greatest need. The politics of Global Development is greater than the geopolitical interests of any one country.

GLOBAL GOAL 16

Peace and Justice and Strong Institutions

Promote peaceful and inclusive societies for sustainable development, provide access to justice for all and build effective, accountable and inclusive institutions at all levels

▷IMPACT|2030

IMPACT 2030 is the only business-led effort designed to marshal the power of employee volunteer investments to advance the achievement of the Global Goals. The IMPACT 2030 coalition convenes leaders from corporations, the United Nations, governments, civil society, academia, and philanthropic organizations from around the world. At the end of our fifteen-year charter, they will leave existing and new organizations with advanced tools to engage employees in volunteer work, measure impact of volunteer efforts, and promote the power of employee volunteers to change the world.

CHAPTER TEN

I'll Fly Away

D ana and I arrived back in the states on a foggy early morning in New York City. The Statue of Liberty held its torch above a thick blanket of moisture, and the sun still hadn't begun to rise. Our arrival signaled the beginning of a new life phase. We were a newly married couple about to begin a new life with high expectations, including those we held for ourselves. I would be the new Third Congressional District Director for Congressman Bonker back in Olympia.

We had both loved Washington, DC, but we wanted to start a family. The nation's capital was addictive, and if we stayed, I would work around the clock. As we packed our car and small rented trailer, we agreed to someday return to DC if the time was right. For now, though, the West was calling.

We drove cross country to Olympia, Washington, our final destination. Our arrival marked the official end of our honeymoon. We pulled up in front of our rental house, and to my surprise, Mom was waiting on the front porch.

During the next couple of years, she would live with us part-time and attend graduate school at St. Martin's College. Mom's schooling in Olympia left Jefferson with the domestic responsibilities in Sequim, namely Jeffie-Lou and Shawne, who were now twelve and fifteen. At age sixty-four, he was finally down to one job, mowing the grass at Dungeness Golf Course. He was enjoying the easier life, and he still preached every Sunday.

After finishing her degree, Mom landed a supervisor's position at the Sequim post office, where she flourished for many years. When I reflect on her life, I realize how amazing Mom's achievements were. She gave up almost everything to escape Dad's violence.

When I look back on the many memories of being with Mom and Jefferson, I still remember the day we went fishing at the pond outside Edwardsville. It stands as one of my fondest memories. So does the day our whole family went to the Michael Jackson Concert Tour in Vancouver, British Columbia. Michael Jackson was spectacular, but my most vivid memory from the night is of watching Jefferson smile throughout the entire show. He always loved music, and at the time Michael Jackson was the best singer on the planet.

I know Jefferson loved us all, but a part of him must have always missed Kansas. We never talked about it. Fifteen months after our trip to Vancouver, he left us forever.

⁓

I was on a business trip when the call came. It was Mom.

"Jefferson has lung cancer. It's terminal." I gasped as Mom spoke.

"What do you mean he has incurable lung cancer? How can that happen?"

"He had a cough and some chest pain, and he went to see Dr. Sims. They took x-rays. Then Dr. Sims came in and said, 'Jefferson you're full of cancer, I don't know what to do,' and he just cried."

I said, "Well, there's gotta be a cure. What happens next?"

"We don't know. We're sending him to Seattle to get some tests."

"How's Jefferson doing?"

"He's okay. Do you want to talk to him?"

"Yes."

"How's my number one son?" Jefferson asked when he got on the phone.

"How are *you* doing?"

"Well the lord giveth and the lord taketh away."

We would take this challenge on together. I flew home as soon as I could. During the next few weeks, we took Jefferson to see specialists at the University of Washington. They gave him less than a year to live. They also offered an experimental radiation therapy reserved for patients with no other options. If it worked, the tumor would stop growing and possibly even shrink. It might prolong his life. But, the doctors explained, it could work the other way, too.

We drove home from Seattle and prayed. Jefferson decided to try the treatment. At first, the tumor shrunk. Then it spread. The cancer metastasized to Jefferson's brain. Then to his spine. We checked him back into the University of Washington Hospital located in Seattle. Jefferson became paralyzed below the waist. It was a Saturday. I remember because he told me he wanted me to go back to Sequim to preach the next morning. I began to protest.

"I don't have a sermon prepared," I said. "I don't know what I would say."

Jefferson looked up from his hospital bed. It was the same look he used to give me when I was a kid and he wanted me to listen carefully. "You don't need a sermon," he said. "You need to prepare your heart."

Jefferson was able to be moved home for hospice care a few days later. There would be no further attempts at treatment. I drove the two hours up from Olympia multiple times a week to help care for him. The church community and others around Sequim also helped. Mom and Jeffie-Lou and Shawne spent as much time as they could at home. Dana took leave from work and moved in full time to help.

A steady stream of visitors flowed in and out of the cabin in the woods. Even in his dying, Jefferson was bringing people together. We moved his bed downstairs to the guest bedroom, which had more room for people to visit now that he was paralyzed. Jefferson officiated a wedding right there. He also started preaching again. Small groups circled around his bed to hear some of his final sermons.

Knowing they would lose their pastor soon, members of the Little Brown Church held Sunday services by his bedside.

I recall one Sunday in particular. We managed to get almost fifty people into his room. Another fifty filled the adjacent dining room. We had a gospel band and special singers. Jefferson projected his voice as loud as he could. By then, it was nearly a whisper. To me, it still sounded as beautiful as it had that first day inside Gethsemane Baptist.

During one of Jefferson's final sermons, a family that didn't normally come to church brought their children to the house to be baptized. It happened without planning. Someone carried a horse trough from outside to the edge of Jefferson's bed, and we filled it with water from a hose. I helped Jefferson as he tried to touch each child for baptism. I didn't even know their names.

Jefferson placed his hand on each of their heads and spoke the eternal words: "May the Lord bless and keep you. May the Lord shine His face upon you. In the name of the Father, the Son, and the Holy Ghost, I baptize you, and you shall have life everlasting. Go in peace, my children."

Drawing of Jefferson with his parrot Moe by Steve Devine

Through his suffering, Jefferson handled himself with courage, love, and humor, even near the bitter end when pain overwhelmed him and he could no longer speak. As his condition worsened, Mom remained by his side around the clock. Jefferson grew weaker by the day. Not once did he complain. As Christmas approached, I knew it would be Jefferson's last. Dana flew back to the East Coast to be with her family. I went to Sequim. Mom and I were so consumed by caring for Jefferson that we forgot to plan Christmas dinner. We dug out some TV dinners and ate together by Jefferson's bed. I remember Mom complaining about stomach cramps. Christmas and the New Year came and went. Jeffie-Lou and Shawne returned to school, and we settled in for the end.

Memories of Jefferson are vivid and fill a lifetime. His last sermon at the Little Brown Church before he was paralyzed was about Psalm 23 "Thou shall not want." His favorite bible verses—and there were many—were "Jesus Wept" and "Suffer not the little children let them come unto me." His favorite benediction: "Let the meditation of my heart be acceptable in thy sight Oh God my Lord and my salvation." His favorite attire during the week: blue overalls. On Sundays: a dark suit, white shirt, and tie.

Before he died, Sydney asked him, "Jefferson, is there anything you would want different?"

His last words to the love of his life were, "Only that we would have had more time together here on Earth as I will love you for eternity."

On February 8, 1986, Jefferson fell into a coma. A doctor visited. Jefferson had already decided he wanted to die naturally at home, and he wouldn't use a respirator or otherwise prolong his life. That same night, Mom collapsed. An ambulance took her to the hospital. She had severe intestinal blockage.

With church members filling the house, I divided the next day between the log cabin and the hospital, as Mom underwent surgery. We moved Jefferson's bed to the living room so more visitors could surround him. He remained in a coma, his breathing faint.

That night with the house nearly empty, I went upstairs to rest. A single church member stationed by Jefferson's bed called my name a few minutes later. I rushed downstairs. Jefferson had motioned slightly with his hand. I sat down beside him and placed one of his hands inside my own. I began to speak.

"Jefferson, it's Scottie. I love you. Mother's okay. Jeffie and Shawne are here with me. We all love you. I love you. I hope you know how much I love you. It's your turn to be at peace. Thank you for all you have done for everyone, especially me. Thank you for teaching me that there is more than anger in this world. I will always try to do good and make you proud."

Jefferson let out the final gasp of air still left in him. Then he was gone.

Reverend Jefferson Jackson died early in the morning. I later learned that Mom woke from surgery at the exact same time. A few days before Jefferson slipped into his coma, I received a call that my paternal grandmother had died. Dad wanted me to come for the funeral. I told him I couldn't. Again, I was forced to make a choice between two families. Again, I chose Jefferson.

Jefferson's funeral took place at the Little Brown Church. Mom dressed Jefferson in a long white robe with golden slippers. Pat Wright and the Total Experience choir performed. Attendees packed the church and flowed out the door into the yard. Dana and I sat in the front row with mom, Shawne, and Jeffie-Lou. I delivered the eulogy and talked about the influence Jefferson had on my life and so many others. I recalled that first day at Gethsemane Baptist when Jefferson's singing overtook me. I talked about our cross-country escape and how Jefferson and Mom fought for my custody in the face of violence and racism.

Jefferson was our rock. My mom loved Jefferson. Jeffie-Lou and Shawne loved Jefferson. I loved Jefferson. Without him, I might never have grown to look beneath the color of a person's skin. Without him, I might never have known that a man doesn't need to be filled with violence and anger to earn respect. Without him, I wouldn't have stayed close to God. He taught me that each of us has a chance to impact others simply by being the best people we can be. He changed the lives of everyone he touched.

After the service, a long procession drove from the church to Sequim View Cemetery. At the gravesite, we all sang "When the Saints Go Marching In." Jefferson was one of those saints. As his body was lowered into the ground, tears flowed and we released hundreds of multicolored balloons into the sky. The closing hymn at the burial was "I'll Fly Away," as the balloons turned to tiny dots, carrying the lyrics, floating above, fading to silence.

> *Some glad morning when this life is o'er, I'll fly away;*
> *To a home on God's celestial shore, I'll fly away.*

Our beloved Jefferson died too early at age sixty-four. Jefferson's grave marker is inscribed on a roughly hewn field rock: "Beloved Husband, Father and Pastor." I chose the name Scott Jackson because I wanted to model my life after Jefferson. It was how he treated others regardless of how they treated him. It was how he truly lived his faith . . . "forbearing and forgiving one another". . . Christ-like.

Jefferson Jackson's grave marker

While I often wondered if my life would have been easier if my parents had stayed together and my father had given me more opportunities in life, I now know that without Jefferson's influence, I could have been a different man—a man more like my dad. Jefferson taught me that it was better to love than to hate. He showed me how to choose forgiveness, to treat women with respect, and to accept people with a different color of skin as equal, even as family. His greatest gift was that he loved me unconditionally.

Jefferson Jackson lived almost his entire life in small towns. He was undereducated. He saw very little of the world.

But he changed it for the better.

Leaving a Legacy

Jefferson didn't finish the tenth grade. He died with very few material possessions. He was ostracized because of the color of his skin. Yet, through his faith and goodness, he left a legacy of hope for all those he touched and for generations to come. His favorite song and my favorite to hear him sing was "I Wonder Do You Love the Lord Like I Do." The meaningful words of this song and the heart and passion with which Jefferson sang them are positive messages I will never forget and try every day to live by. They encouraged me to choose a career path in philanthropy.

> *I wonder, do you, love the Lord as I do. What he gave to me was given to you.*
>
> *Are you staying here content. Will your soul some day repent.*
>
> *Will you show a child the way. Will you do your best even in distress.*
>
> *Will you do some good each day. I wonder, do you.*

Since 2014 we have seen record-breaking years for private philanthropy, with an estimated $358 billion raised. Giving in the United States has now surpassed the previous pre-recession high water mark of $355 billion in 2007. While individuals still account for more than 70 percent of all philanthropic contributions, giving is growing across all categories—individuals, bequests, foundations, and corporations. International causes saw the largest increase in giving with $5.1 billion in 2015. Still, less than 5 percent of those who contribute give to international causes. We are anticipated to be entering the golden age of philanthropy in which several trillion dollars are expected to change hands and generations of donors.

Philanthropy itself is changing and evolving. Philanthropy in its broadest terms includes time, talent, and treasure. An increasing number of donors not only give to individual nonprofits but also to issues, land causes, and organizations they believe are having the greatest impact on the issues they care about. The continuum of philanthropy and/or social impact investments now spans individual gifts, foundation grants, and program-related investments, corporate contributions, gifts in kind of products and services, skill-based volunteerism, impact investing, social enterprises, and business-aligned or market-based solutions to social problems.

Partnerships cut across public, private, and nonprofit sectors. Increasingly, LLCs and for-profit business structures are being set up to direct philanthropy, just as businesses are utilizing not-for-profit enterprises to generate "shared value" and are displaying "creative capitalism" to odd run social issues. We often now hear terms like triple-bottom line and tri-sector intelligence.

Philanthropists themselves—both institutional and individual—are also changing. The reasons for giving are different between generations, gender, and nationality. Faith-based donors have different motivations than non-faith-based giving. Donors across all categories want to see more impact, and they demand to be personally connected to the causes they care about.

For the international sector not only are women and girls the largest category of vulnerable people in the world, but women donors have also become the most dominant donor for global causes. As we focus on donors who will support the Global Goals for Sustainability over the next fifteen years, we must build relationships with younger generations. While there has been considerable attention given to millennials, there has also been a growing body of evidence that we should be paying even more attention to who will be our next immediate group of donors. For the international sector future giving will be in the hands, hearts, and minds of Generation Xers and older millennials, and of most importance the 30–45-year-old female donors who have the weight of the world on their shoulders. These women are interested in seeing the world change for the better and for those close to them.

Strategic philanthropy is becoming the norm. While donors are still willing to take risks, they no longer want to just hand over their contribution without knowing more details about the process. They want to understand strategy, market disruption, innovation, return on investment, and leverage factor to others contributions, and they all share the desire to see measurable impact.

Across all of these trends, giving with purpose is no longer a phenomenon in the United States or a select number of countries with tax deduction eligibility. Giving is global, and no one can escape the need to partner. No longer can governments, multilateral institutions, foundations, corporations, or individual donors do it alone if they are to achieve a legacy of impact. Individual country donors and multi-lateral donors, such as the Global Fund, the World Bank, the World Health Organization, and even the United Nations, have all formed strategic alliances and partnerships with private sector institutional and individual donors, and vice versa.

Our ability as humanity to achieve the Global Goals depends on how well we achieve Goal #17 "Partnerships for the Goals." We must forge partnerships between governments, non-governmental organizations, businesses, and individuals. We must create partnerships for providing financial resources, technology, capacity building, trade, measuring impact, and answers to systemic societal issues.

Global Impact has had the opportunity to partner with Impact 2030, our charity and corporate partners, and we have even set up a Sustainable Development Goals Fund for both workplace giving and for individual donors.

Bill Gates, cofounder of Microsoft, is currently the world's richest individual, with an estimated worth of over $85 billion dollars. Bill and Melinda Gates are also two of the world's largest philanthropists. The Bill & Melinda Gates Foundation (BMGF), the world's largest private foundation, commits in grants as much as three billion dollars per year and has granted over the course of its short lifespan more than $26 billion in grants for developing and deploying lifesaving vaccines, for eradicating polio, eliminating malaria, finding new models and scalable solutions for preventing child morbidity and mortality, improving maternal and child health, investing in women, improving agricultural yields for small farmers in Africa, and investing in education in the United States.

The Bill & Melinda Gates Foundation has also brought together more than 1,500 of the world's best minds as full-time staff members to work on how to solve these problems. All of this is done in partnership with not-for-profit grantees, government, global leaders, celebrities, the private sector, other foundations, and individual philanthropists worldwide. I have had the privilege throughout my career to watch and work with BMGF and support their partnerships in philanthropy, programs, and policy change in their belief that all lives matter and that all human beings are equal and deserve an opportunity to realize their potential and live healthy lives.

Perhaps the Gates Foundation's greatest legacy, including that of Bill Gates Senior, was when they joined forces with Warren Buffet to encourage other philanthropists to contribute the majority of their resources and have an impact on the world's most pressing issues in their lifetime. Beginning with the Giving Pledge, philanthropists in the United States and around the world have taken the pledge to commit their wealth in their lifetime to change the world.

Mark Zuckerberg, cofounder and chief executive of Facebook, together with his wife, Dr. Priscilla Chan, in an open letter to their newborn daughter, Max, made a commitment to give 99 percent of their Facebook shares during their lifetime—currently worth more than $45 billion dollars—to charitable purposes. They plan to fulfill the commitment not just through traditional philanthropy but through a limited liability (LLC) corporate structure that will allow them to realize social impact through both investments and charitable contributions.

The Chan/Zuckerberg initiative represents the new thinking and approaches of a new generation of philanthropists, being modeled by a number of Silicon Valley entrepreneurs and enterprises. Jeff Skoll, founder of Ebay; Marc Benioff, CEO of Salesforce.com; and corporations such as Google, Apple, Unilever, and many others have also made commitments to innovative forms of philanthropy. They are increasingly doing this work in partnership with other philanthropists, such as Michael Bloomberg and Bill Gates. The collective legacy of these collaborations in philanthropy is a good sign for achieving the Global Goals for Sustainability.

Perhaps the greatest challenge and opportunity for realizing the 17 Global Goals for Sustainability and their individual targets will be the role the private sector itself will play and how it will meet the needs of four billion people who represent the untapped number at the base of the pyramid. These four billion individuals have incomes below $3,000 in local purchasing power. Yet together they represent a $45-trillion-dollar marketplace. Whether it is through shared value, creative capitalism, impact investing, social enterprise, or business solutions to bring new technologies and access to food, nutrition, water, good health, clean energy, and economic opportunity, it all relies on whether strategic philanthropy can activate and include the private sector. The Sustainable Development Goals are already serving as a guide and compass for encouraging businesses to take action.

For each of us as Global Citizens, our legacy will depend on how well we connect our own personal stories and journeys to the goals and to the role that each of us can play as a game changer to do our part to change the world in our lifetime. Two young women close to me have especially touched my heart with their own journeys and the choices they have made to choose the charity within and make the world better.

Jeni, the daughter of my close friend John, has chosen a road less traveled. Although she comes from a well-to-do family and has many opportunities, she has opted to work with children who are less fortunate and has committed herself to social good and global development. Jeni now works for Global Impact but her journey has taken her to Zambia to work with AIDS orphans, to Tanzania and South Africa to work with communities and social entrepreneurs, and now back in the

United States to promote social justice and raise resources for those who were born into more difficult circumstances at no fault of their own.

In Jeni's own words: "John F. Kennedy once said: 'As we express our gratitude, we must never forget that the higher appreciation is not to utter words, but to love by them.' My dad said this same thing every night at the dinner table when he reminded us to always be thankful. I probably would have supported international development in some way after coming in contact with poverty for the first time when I was seventeen in Zambia. However, it was my gratitude for the lessons that I have learned through the people working in this space that has made it my passion. Simply put, the great lesson I have encountered came from those who do good because it feels good to do so."

The other young woman is my own daughter, Lindsay Jackson. Here is a small glimpse of Lindsay's story: "I am proud to say that I am what they call a millennial—a product of Generation Y. This distinct generation is classified as being optimists, with a strong hope for the future. We are known to be the most connected, diverse, and collaborative generation to date. We bring a new personality to the table, where we celebrate a citizen-driven society, non-governmental institutions, and a networked approach to solve problems. We value innovation and take full advantage of the opportunity to reimagine.

Every generation carries elements of their generational influence with them in order to make a lasting impact, and lucky for me I had the opportunity to learn from some of the most inspirational individuals, whom I am honored to be able to call my mentors, including my parents. My parents presented me with opportunities to learn through firsthand experiences, where they believed my inspiration would come from my own personal connections. So, they sent me off to Africa.

As a 15-year-old, I was convinced that my adolescent summer was ruined, but little did I know that this was more than a typical family vacation, and that my personal encounter with the effects of AIDS and poverty would not only pave the way but also define the direction of my life. Africa was a land full of contradictions, where the continent's beauty surrounded me with its endless rolling hills and a savanna dotted with exotic wildlife with rich brilliant colors across the horizon, but yet, throughout Africa most people live on less than a dollar per day."

Both of these young women illustrate not only why it's important to get involved but also how it has been meaningful in their own lives. Whether you are a millennial, Gen-Xer, or baby boomer, it's never too late to leave a legacy.

GLOBAL GOAL 17

Partnerships for the Goals

Strengthen the means of implementation and revitalize the global partnership for sustainable development

A successful sustainable development agenda requires partnerships between governments, the private sector, and civil society. These inclusive partnerships built upon principles and values, a shared vision, and shared goals that place people and the planet at the center, are needed at the global, regional, national, and local levels.

GLOBAL IMPACT®

Growing global philanthropy

Global Impact stands at the crossroads of global philanthropy. We work closely on a daily basis with global corporations and international charities to develop partnerships, help charities increase their funding, and assist corporations with their corporate social responsibility initiatives and philanthropy.

Growfund was built to democratize philanthropy. It is absolutely free to join and it's yours to keep throughout your lifetime. There is no minimum contribution, funds are invested immediately, and the minimum amount required to grant is only $25.

Text Source: https://sdgfunds.charity.org/

CHAPTER ELEVEN

The Charity Within

J efferson Jackson may not have traveled the world, but his influence led me to ultimately choose a career path that would not only lead to visiting more than 65 countries but also engaging in meaningful work that would help others in need throughout the world. I kept my promise to him that I would always try to *do good and make him proud.* Jefferson was always there for young people, offering support and guidance to any child in need. I took that to heart and decided to be a force for good to other kids, the way he had been for me.

I worked for Congressman Bonker for half a decade, focusing on international trade and development issues. After Congressman Bonker left office, I formed my own public affairs and marketing company, which included Congressman Bonker, called Tradec (Trade and Development Consortium). And for the next decade, I worked in international public affairs in the private sector, opening new markets in developing countries, before accepting a position at World Vision and moving over to the humanitarian side. At World Vision I helped design programs that would engage our donors and traveled around the world to work with our teams on the ground. I then went on to take a leadership role at PATH, which focused on global health, such as procuring and providing an affordable meningitis vaccine, MenAfriVac®, for Africa.

Now, as the President and CEO of Global Impact, an organization focused on changing the world by growing Global philanthropy, I'm still involved in raising funds and awareness to meet critical humanitarian needs around the world by providing corporations and individual donors with effective ways to donate to international causes and crises. Global Impact's mission is to raise resources for the world's most vulnerable people, and in this capacity I still get to work with World Vision, PATH, and many other international relief and development organizations. In conjunction with our member charities, we work to end hunger, improve prenatal and childhood health care, supply clean water, deliver medicine and other disease-prevention programs, build schools and train teachers, help with rescue efforts following a disaster, and much more. Over the past decade before the great recession, the United States and many other governments have increased public and private sector support for development tenfold. As a result, we have halved child morbidity and mortality, we have actually started to win our assault on deadly but preventable diseases like malaria, and we have turned the tide on the HIV/AIDS pandemic. Yet there is so much more work to be done.

My work has been a surprisingly transformational journey—while I've witnessed firsthand its positive effect on others, the very people we have helped have also had a profound impact on me. I have seen the best in people in the worst conditions and have been deeply moved by their courage and perseverance. So many people helped me when I was a child, and now I've had the privilege of traveling the world and meeting other kids like me.

One of my early trips with World Vision involved co-leading a pastors' trip to the West Bank and Gaza. World Vision was raising funds to support children because it was a conflict-torn area. Some of our donors had supported Palestinian Christians, but many were not fully aware of the dynamics on the ground. I don't think any of us had a real understanding of what was occurring in the Palestinian territories. Our trip was during one of the Intifadas when Arafat was still in power. I had no idea that Palestinians were in such dire straits and being held captive through a series of checkpoints. The checkpoints were every so many hundreds of feet inside Gaza or the West Bank, and if you didn't have the right identification, you couldn't travel past the checkpoint. Palestinians might have a day pass to go to work during the week, but then they were unable to pass the checkpoint on weekends to shop at the grocery store. Towns were literally divided in half.

During our visit, we realized that people were being held here in severe conditions. While inside the West Bank, I stayed with a family that World Vision was sponsoring, and their son gave me a tour of the town. His ability to marry would depend on whether or not he was able to own land and build a home, which under the circumstances was highly unlikely. Everything became affected by the situation they were in: school, nutrition, livelihood—even the ability to marry and have a family. We visited a checkpoint with Palestinian guards where the previous night the Israeli army had mistakenly shot a donkey on that side of the sand bank.

"What if we just go back inside the checkpoint here?" I suggested nervously to the boy who was both my host and interpreter.

We also visited a school for the deaf in the Gaza strip that was supported by World Vision. Because it was so difficult to have a normal community development model, World Vision provided aid to existing institutions, and our visits helped us to determine their funding needs.

Suddenly, an outbreak occurred in the street with gunshots. This provoked the Israeli army on the other side of the boundary to start firing their weapons, and bullets began whizzing by us. We were on the rooftop of the deaf school, and we grabbed the students and marched them downstairs. We tried to transport them safely to their homes through difficult streets, doing our best to avoid the gunfire. The donors and pastors on our trip were all transformed by what they witnessed. Hopefully, we gave some hope to those we visited.

Children at the school for the deaf in Gaza

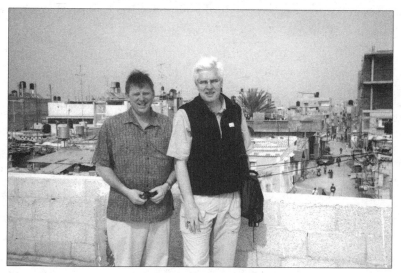

Scott with Rich Stearns, President of World Vision, in Gaza

I will never forget our World Vision trip to Guatemala. We were bringing donors out into the communities where World Vision was working to show them our programs in action, and the sponsorship coordinator urged us to visit a family who had recently lost their daughter. Even though this little girl had received support from World Vision, not every child makes it—a lesson that remains with me today. For every billion who live on less than two dollars a day, many drink bad water, and many of those people die from preventable causes, such as diarrhea. We read about statistics every day, but sometimes we forget that behind that statistic is an actual real, live, human person. Even if we're able to help hundreds or thousands, we are painfully aware that so many do not survive, and they leave behind grieving families.

I met Lesbia Arana, who had lost her daughter Marcia to lupus nine days earlier. Through her tears of grief, Lesbia recounted Marcia's long and painful struggle against her disease, and her need to obtain more and more treatments. Many parents in Guatemala were turned away from doctors because they were poor. World Vision provided Marcia with the best treatment available in the region, but it wasn't enough. We should have been able to do more and we all felt it. Marcia was yet one more statistic, one more child out of so many who would never realize her potential.

What made this particular trip so meaningful was the opportunity I had to engage with Lesbia and how she connected with me. Toward the end of her story about her daughter, I got up out of my seat and put my arms around Lesbia.

"You did everything you could," I said. "She's with the Lord now. We'll take her story back with us and tell others. We won't forget her."

Even though Marcia had died, we could still take her story and do something with it. She could serve as a reminder of how far we had yet to come and why we needed to remain committed to this work.

The success stories are important because they give us hope, but the kids who don't make it serve as a haunting reminder.

When I was working with PATH, I took a trip to Vietnam with a group of donors. We were there to see the work PATH was implementing around the country. PATH is an organization that works with pharmaceutical companies around the world and creates health technologies for low-income communities, simple things that could be used in health clinics with minimal training. They had just invented a vaccination syringe that could be used by anyone, not only medical professionals, which would enable more people to receive vaccinations.

We visited one health clinic in a community where PATH had been involved with training. It was vaccination day, and there was a nurse on site. At least one hundred women were lined up, and each held her child's vaccination card. They were there to receive the vaccinations for that particular month, and people had traveled from rural communities in Hanoi in the northern part of Vietnam. We entered the clinic and observed the vaccinations and then saw the sharp waste. In addition to the problem of people reusing needles, they often discard needles in places where no one will take them away and safely dispense of them. In many cases, huge piles of needles accumulate and form treacherous mounds next to these clinics. Kids play with them, and it's a nightmare.

PATH invented a system for detaching the needle from the rest of the vaccine, cutting down waste, and then stacking the needles within a container that could hold thousands of needles—like a big barrel with a top that had a special opening for the waste. This container could then be buried in the ground as a way to safely eliminate this waste and protect people from getting hurt. These seemingly small inventions can have a huge impact on health and safety in third world communities.

I pulled the nurse on staff aside and said, "Can you tell me what impact PATH has had on your clinic? What else can we be doing?"

She replied, "PATH has brought life-saving vaccines to our clinic. PATH has trained us and given us the tools and equipment to have a well-running clinic to serve more people. And, finally, as a result, PATH has helped to make our community healthy and prosperous."

The PATH trips were a bit more indirect, because we weren't actually running the clinic itself. The work of PATH was more about training and developing appropriate technologies in health that could then be implemented in communities where it was needed. But it was important for donors to see firsthand how PATH was improving people's lives. The donors were appreciative of the experience and it affected each of them differently. Some were struck by the fact that it had helped communities, others that children were kept alive.

As a father, it was important to me to share some of these experiences with my daughters. I wanted to broaden their perspectives and show them how other people lived around the world. I also wanted to impart the lesson that helping those less fortunate was a valuable action and something they could aspire to in their own lives.

While working at World Vision, I had the opportunity to take my eldest daughter Lindsay, who was about twelve at the time, on a medical boat that traveled up and down the tributaries of the Amazon River in South America. For many villages, the only regular medical care they received was from one of these medical boats. We lived on the boat for a week, along with some of World Vision's donors. We witnessed everything from standard vaccination days to more severe heart attacks and strokes, as well as triage for the sick. The boat would stay overnight in one area and then move on to the next community the following day.

From this experience, we all began to comprehend the real importance of health care, especially for kids. It was interesting for me to see
my daughter Lindsay realize the significance of having clean water
in a place that had very little drinkable water and take an interest in
testing the water. We recognized the juxtaposition of the breathtak-
ing Milky Way at night and lush environment during the day with
the stark contrast of so much pollution due to a lack of sanitation. But
Lindsay's real epiphany would come on our next trip.

A couple years later, I took the family with me on a trip to Africa,
including my three daughters. We started off in South Africa and
then traveled to Zambia and Kenya.

We visited a small Catholic hospice dedicated to people dying
of AIDS, unable to receive life-saving treatment because of poverty.
Once HIV was contracted, there was no hope. Their final days were
spent at this hospice. The first two rooms contained orphaned babies
and toddlers, and we held the babies in our arms. The reality of their
condition struck all of us, especially Lindsay. They were alone, dying,
and there was no hope of treatment; and yet they still managed to
express happiness through their laughter and singing. In the final two
rooms, adults occupied each bed and all available floor space. Emaci-
ated, sick, and saddened faces peered at us from above their meager
blankets. One man had traveled a great distance to die alone, so as
not to be a burden or stigma to his family and village.

We were also able to see some of our work in action in the Shipanuka community in Zambia, where we celebrated the funding that
had given them a new well and latrines. We all had a huge feast
together, and then they took us to see the new wells. We did a ribbon
cutting for the latrines, and they introduced us to two twin girls who
were the same age as our twins.

In a hotel in the capital city of Lusaka in Zambia, Lindsay had a life-changing experience. It was early evening, and Lindsay was in the room, freshening up before dinner, when an African housekeeper entered to clean the room. As she began to empty the trash, she pulled out a candy wrapper that had been discarded by one of the twins, with a couple pieces of candy still remaining.

The woman looked at Lindsay and said, "Do you mind? Are you going to eat this? There are two candies left inside. Why did you throw them away?"

"No, I don't mind," Lindsay replied. "My sisters threw it away."

"If you don't mind, I will take it home to my children because they don't have candy. We don't have food to spare here, and every little bit counts."

In Africa, most people live on less than a dollar per day. This intimate one-on-one encounter made Lindsay fully realize what this meant. What many of us discard in life, someone else can hold precious.

The Jackson girls meet twin counterparts from Shipanuka, Zambia

The Jackson girls, Lindsay, Haley, and Allison, surrounded by the children of Shipanuka, Zambia

When I moved over to the humanitarian side, I saw things I would never have seen otherwise. These experiences helped me to see the human face of our work and why it matters to children around the world. What drives me is that while in some respects it feels so far away, from my own childhood I know that what other people do to create opportunity means that kids like me get an education, medical care, and what they need. I never had to live on a dollar a day. But I did grow up in a tenuous house where I felt real fear as a child, and when I finally escaped I was confronted with racism and poverty. I worked hard to improve my circumstances, but the generosity of so many people helped me along the way.

As a kid it really meant something to have others express confidence in me and to believe that I had potential. I was grateful for the programs that allowed our family to make ends meet or enabled me to have an education. The opportunities I received because of the generosity of others, as well as the institutions for social good, had a

Women members of the microcredit farming cooperative in Swaziland

real and lasting impact on me. There are so many children in this world who come from broken homes and don't ever have the chance to realize their potential. Some don't even make it to school or receive any type of health care. Because of the positive influences in my life like Jefferson and my mom, I learned to view life with a sense of optimism and to do my best regardless of circumstances. As an adult I've chosen to love people and be positive—and my own childhood has caused me to be drawn to marginalized people around the world.

I don't think it's a coincidence that I've met so many other kids like me during my travels, children who were around the same age that I was when I made my own escape. I'm not looking for credit—that's not important to me; I only care about what we all accomplish to help these children. I believe that each of us will be measured by what we do or don't do to eradicate extreme poverty so that every child can realize his or her potential. I know firsthand how important that is. We all have charity within. For me, it's about choosing love instead of anger or hate.

Advocating to Eliminate Extreme Poverty

Half the world lives on less than two dollars and fifty cents a day. More than two billion live on less than two dollars a day. Can you imagine this? Sixty-six percent of the world's work force is comprised of women who earn only 10 percent of the world's income. We have the opportunity to eliminate extreme poverty in our lifetime. To achieve this audacious global goal of eliminating extreme poverty, we must have clear intentions for providing economic opportunity, the means to have basic food and nutrition, and access to health care for everyone.

There are 842 million hungry people in the world, and 98 percent of them live in less developed countries. In some countries and communities, unemployment exceeds 50 percent of the population. The scale of such economic uncertainty, especially when underemployment is factored into the numbers, means that a large percentage of the world's most vulnerable people are without the means of a viable livelihood for themselves or for their families.

Poor nutrition is the cause of nearly half the deaths of children, totaling more than 3.1 million child deaths each year. Sixty percent of the world's hungry are women. Being poor is the greatest indicator of hunger and vice versa. It is projected that if women farmers had access to the same resources and financial means as men, the number of hungry people in the world could be reduced by as many as 150 million.

Nearly one billion people lack access to safe water. Women in developing countries spend 20 million hours a day each year collecting water. Every 21 seconds a child dies from a water-borne illness. More people die from unsanitary drinking water than all forms of violent conflict and war. The World Health Organization estimates that 36 million die each year from water-related diseases. More people in the world have cell phones than toilets.

Bono of the band U2 visited Philadelphia in 2004 as part of the ONE Campaign. It has been a personal mission of his to advocate to eliminate extreme poverty and hunger ever since he experienced both in Ethiopia during the famine in the 1980s when World Vision had the privilege of hosting Bono as he visited the camps. Bono, a person of faith, has never wavered in his commitment to eradicate poverty. He wouldn't remember me, but I was in the room when he told the original NGO partners of the ONE Campaign To Make Poverty History, "I am just a voice for those who have none. I can do what I do because you have my back! Because you are on the front lines, taking care of those in need and breaking the cycle of poverty so that everyone can realize their potential."

The next morning, he was wearing his famous tinted glasses and a camouflage shirt. With little sleep, he still looked cooler than all of us in our suits, who were there with him to launch the "ONE Campaign" in front of the Liberty Bell on May 16, 2004. The next year *TIME* magazine named him person of the year, together with Bill and Melinda Gates. I was proud of the part I had played in uniting three different campaigns with the support of Joe Cerrell of the Gates Foundation, as they all became the ONE Campaign to Make Poverty History.

More recently, the Global Citizen Campaign has brought Beyonce, JZ, and Coldplay to advocate for the world's most vulnerable.

In September 2015, many of these advocates came together in Central Park to give voice to those in extreme poverty. I was there with my Board Chair Steve Polo and contingent from Global Impact. Comic Relief, the U.K.'s most visible public charity, brought Red Nose Day to the United States to raise more than $23 million dollars for charities in the United States and around the world. In addition to my staff taping me to a pole in a onesie clown suit to raise money for Red Nose, Global Impact serves as the US Partnerships Coordinator to raise resources and advocate for the end of extreme poverty.

The Global Citizen Festival and Advocacy Campaign spokespeople like Beyonce, Lady Gaga, Bono, and Cold Play, the Clinton Global Initiative, Impact 2030, the ONE Campaign, Global Impact, and many other organizations and individuals are helping to increase the visibility of the Global Goals, but it is still not enough. Each and every one of us on the planet has to make a commitment to these goals. It is not enough for China to pledge $60 million for development that supports their investments in Africa and around the world. We must all be a voice and advocate for more funds to reach the most vulnerable and those countries in greatest need.

GLOBAL GOALS 1, 2, 6, and 7

- *End poverty in all its forms everywhere*
- *End hunger, achieve food security and improved nutrition and promote sustainable agriculture*
- *Ensure availability and sustainable management of water and sanitation for all*
- *Ensure access to affordable, reliable, sustainable and modern energy for all*

Growing global philanthropy

In the UK, Red Nose Day has been going on since 1988 and is an inspiring cultural phenomenon that unites people from all walks of life in the interest of saving and changing lives across the globe. In 2015 Red Nose Day launched in the USA with Global Impact as a key fundraising partner. NBC, Walgreens, and Mars brought together celebrities, musicians, corporate partners, and the public and raised more than $23 million to help lift children out of poverty. In 2016 Red Nose Day raised over $34 million with Global Impact once again acting as a key fundraising partner.

Charities in Action

Comic Relief is the organizer of Red Nose Day, driving positive change through the power of entertainment. They tackle the root causes of poverty and social injustice across the world.

The ONE Campaign seeks to raise public awareness and work with political leaders to combat AIDS and preventable diseases, increase investments in agriculture and nutrition, and demand greater transparency of governments.

CHAPTER TWELVE

To Gulu and Back

In late 2005, I led a humanitarian trip to central Africa that had the most profound impact upon me. It was the center of a vicious and horrible civil war between the people of Northern Uganda and the Lord's Liberation Army (LLA), led by deranged warlord Joseph Kony. For nearly two decades, Kony had been kidnapping, raping, and enslaving local children. The Acholi people of northern Uganda and South Sudan have absorbed the brunt of Kony's genocide. More than 1.5 million Acholi are considered internally displaced persons (IDPs) and for their own protection are now forced to live in overcrowded refugee camps, enduring squalid conditions. They live in constant fear of invasion of their villages and communities by the young, brainwashed warriors of the LLA.

Kony was known for raiding villages before dawn, abducting young boys into submission to become soldiers, raping girls, and forcing them into slavery until he discarded them later on the trail—beaten to death or maimed beyond recognition. Beatings alone did not suffice. The LLA has made its mark by lopping off the arms, legs, breasts, noses, and ears of the victims. They especially practice these brutal methods of control on the young girls and children. To avoid these atrocities, the families in the surrounding villages and region encourage their children to make their way into the city of Gulu, where the United Nations and the participating nongovernmental organizations (NGOs) maintain secured compounds with separate makeshift barracks for the boys and girls.

The "night walkers," as these school-aged children are known, make their way into the city before dusk to study by flood lights, sleep, and then by the first light of dawn return to their family homes for a meal of meager proportions. These children then travel to the village school, and the cycle begins all over again. This nightly ritual continues as long as there is known LLA activity in the region. Kony and his child soldiers seek refuge across the border in Sudan, where the Muslim extremist government seems to tolerate their ungodly cause. Over the past twenty years, the LLA has captured, brainwashed, maimed, or discarded for dead more than twenty thousand innocent children. These children are the unlucky ones. The lucky ones—the night walkers—simply live in fear. But they live.

I arrived in Kampala, the capitol of Uganda, after a long flight and taxi ride from the Kampala airport to downtown Gulu. The rest of my delegation, which consisted of Rotarians, donors, and community leaders who wanted to witness World Vision's work, arrived late that same day. At the time, I was a senior vice president of World Vision, the world's largest nonprofit relief and development organization. The Seattle delegation was a unique group of individuals. They had recently witnessed polio vaccinations in Ethiopia. But nothing they saw in Ethiopia, nor anything I had seen in the more than 65 countries and difficult places around the world I had traveled to, could have prepared us for what we experienced in Gulu.

The next morning we boarded our chartered bus outside the hotel for our journey to Gulu, two hundred miles north. It was a bumpy ride. As we moved farther from the capital, the roads grew rougher, cars became infrequent, and the landscape faded into rural settlements. At various points along the way, bicycles crowded beside us, and women circled us with baskets, overflowing in color, balanced perfectly on their heads. We encountered more frequent checkpoints as we headed north. As we crossed the halfway point, closer to Gulu than to Kampala, we knew Kony's army was near by the heightened presence of government troops. We distracted ourselves by thinking about the children of Gulu, the victims we hoped to help.

The final checkpoint on the long, winding road before we reached the city took a long time. Government soldiers surrounded the bus. Two boarded with their machine guns visible, briefly speaking to the driver, deciding whether or not our delegation could continue. We realized that the conflict here, while deep-seated, was also very real and evident. We were finally allowed to proceed but only after one of the soldiers had walked up and down the aisle and was satisfied that the contents of the bus, including the delegation members, were not to be worried about.

Nothing could have prepared us for what we were about to witness.

Gulu resembled a walled-in city—without an actual wall. In its attempt to protect inhabitants from Joseph Kony, the city sealed itself off from the rest of the world. Driving toward our hotel, we saw signs of war on every block. Army transport trucks. United Nations Refugee Commission supply vehicles. World Food Programme warehouses. And, of course, the large football field-like enclosures with makeshift barracks and floodlights where the night walkers would seek refuge. Our hotel in Gulu was rudimentary, even compared to Kampala, with clean rooms but no electricity or hot water. The beds sported mosquito nets, an important amenity during malaria season.

We spent the next several days learning, listening, and witnessing the results of the war atrocities firsthand. We also saw the hope for a better future in the faces of the Gulu children and people we met—those who had been left behind. Women were still not outside of harm's way in the massive refugee camps, as many were raped inside the camps as a matter of course. We met with Acholi tribal leaders who were powerless because they were significantly outnumbered against the well-armed LLA young vanguard.

Our delegation had an extraordinary experience visiting and spending the day with the maimed, disfigured, but ever so hopeful women taking refuge in the World Vision Children of War Rehabilitation Center for former child soldiers and the women and young girls who managed to escape the LLA. The center provided them with food, medical treatment, psychological counseling, and vocational training, among other things. These children came to the center before they would then try to travel home to their villages, many of them traumatized and lacking the ability to reintegrate themselves into their communities. Some of them would never be able to live independently or return to their family homes. Some had babies; some were just kids.

I met a young woman whose nose had been cut off. One of her breasts had been sliced off and she was missing an arm, with only a stump in its place. She was only twelve or fourteen and had been fetching water when the army captured her and forced her brother into military service. But she was still alive, and I saw the love she carried for her son, the bastard child of the man who had raped and maimed her. She sat down on her bunk in a small room with her baby on her lap and began to tell me her story through an interpreter. I sat with the woman a long time. And as I listened to her story, her son played nearby.

When she was captured, she was raped multiple times and then given to a much older soldier as a trophy bride. One night when the soldiers weren't paying much attention, she tried to escape. They cut off her nose, breasts, and ears, so that she would be too ugly and damaged to receive help. She gave birth to a child but never knew which soldier had fathered it. A few months after she gave birth, fighting erupted and the LLA army was losing, so it retreated and she fled. The Uganda government army rescued her and brought her to the World Vision rehabilitation center in Gulu. There were a million other refugees. I told her she was brave and beautiful—truly beautiful

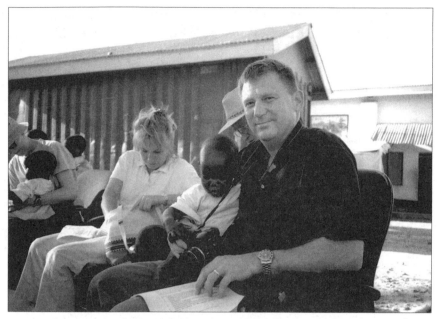

Scott with a child at the World Vision Children of War Rehabilitation Center

inside and out. She smiled and thanked me. She would do more than survive. World Vision would see to that.

We then went outside and took a picture of our delegation with all of the women because they wanted us to. We listened intently to their stories and spent time with them, just as others had been with me during my difficult times. These women had been through so much—and yet they had endured and found their own charity within, including love for their fatherless children, born out of violence and rape. As they shared their love, we shared in return. We felt joy for the triumph of the human spirit.

Later that afternoon, the World Vision staff had arranged for me to visit my sponsored child, Simon Ojok. World Vision is the largest child sponsorship agency in the world. Simon was only one year older than our twin girls, Haley and Allison, and three years younger than our oldest daughter Lindsay. The girls, when they were still young, had chosen Simon's picture when we decided to sponsor a child while attending our first World Vision Child sponsorship concert in September 2000. It was during intermission, and we selected Simon in war-torn Northern Uganda. Or perhaps as I stood in front of a photograph of Simon and his family, he picked us.

We sponsored Simon for more than a decade, during most of his precious and precarious childhood. Every year we received a picture of Simon and a report on his progress. And every year I had been thankful that he was still alive. Now I fully understood the real possibility that Simon could easily become a victim. Simon could have been a night walker. His brothers and sisters, who were older, could have also been night walkers.

Simon lived in the nearby village, and we drove an hour to visit him in our white Land Rover with the bright orange World Vision decals on the side. As we drew closer, the roads began to give way to rough terrain. Finally, we pulled up to a hut with a grass roof, and Simon and his mother and brother came out to greet us. Simon lived with his siblings and his mother—his father was no longer living. He was very shy and I shook his hand, as the interpreter told him who I was and he in turn expressed his appreciation. I explained that my family had been supporting him for a long time, helping him get to school and receive medical help. He told me that he wanted to be a construction worker. First he had wanted to be a teacher, then a construction worker, and then a hairdresser. When he completed elementary school, he asked World Vision to help him pay for vocational school—he wanted a profession so that he could take care of his mom, who had become HIV positive.

They invited me into their hut, and his mom was so proud of having us there. Simon pulled out a box that contained a few of the letters we had sent him over the years, so I knew he understood who we were. I had brought some school supplies, books, clothes, a soccer ball, and a Polaroid camera—simple gifts for a family who needed so much. It had been all I had been able to carry with me. It reminded me of when I could only bring my deflated basketball, when I had been forced to determine what was most important to me and what I would have to leave behind in my efforts to escape my abusive father. Everything we do counts for somebody.

Simon is now more than 21 years old. We continued to help sponsor Simon during vocational school, until his mother became ill and he was required to return home to support her and the family. Sadly, we have recently lost track of Simon. When we met in person that time, it was somewhat awkward. And yet there was a connection that we could not deny. Simon was a survivor and so was I. Simon

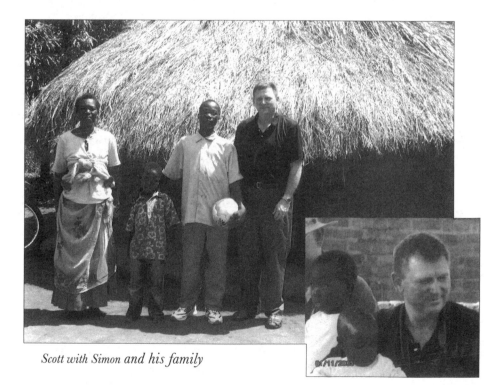

Scott with Simon and his family

though a seemingly ordinary boy was—by staying alive, staying in school, and supporting his mom—without knowing it, living an extraordinary life as a model for all of humanity. At one point Simon sent me a letter that I will forever cherish. It was not unlike the letters I have sent to the people who have looked after me, the individuals who saw something in me that triggered the charity within them. Without their help, I would not have made it across the country to be with my mom, I would not have finished college, and I would not have had an opportunity to provide for my family and try to make a difference in the world. Simon's letter sent on October 3, 2012 reminds me of those letters and those significant others in my life:

Dear Scott,

First of all I would like to send my greeting to all of your family members. How are you out there? It has been a very grateful happiness when I and my mother heard that you sent school fees. It has been a God plan for me to have school fees. I always put my trust in God as the Bible says. God has done a great miracle for in my life to have studies and I promise that I will never spoil my opportunity to do so.

Honestly, I received the money and paid for my fees and also I bought with the fees other school requirements such as a ream of printing paper, A4 figure log table, a drawing board, T-Square, a mathematical set, half a dozen of 96 page exercise books, 3 meter tape measure, 3 kgs of welding rod, 10 hacksaw blades (eclipses) 18 teeth per 20 mm, 3 drill bits (size 4), and 6 toilet rolls (required for boarding students).

Scott, thank you for your cooperation over my studies. Please send my greetings to all your family members. I have to stop here thanks. Blessings to almighty God.

Thanks,
Ojok Simon

The war was at a precarious state. Every night was different. Some nights there were few night walkers and the streets were relatively empty; other nights when the LLA activity was sighted nearby, there were many thousands of child night walkers. That evening our delegation would walk in solidarity with whoever walked to Gulu in search of refuge.

Just before dusk, the streets lay empty. Then small dark faces began to emerge in the twilight. They seemed to materialize from nowhere. Soon, a sea of children surrounded us, crowding onto every path coming into the city. Thousands of bodies pushed against each other as we moved toward the stadium, the epicenter of safety. In the midst of the crowd, I felt a tug on my hand. I looked down and saw a young girl. She said her name was Rose, and she asked who I was and where I came from. She smiled at me, gave me her hand, and we moved together with the mass.

Rose and I, along with the rest of our delegation, made our way, seemingly pushed along by the crowds of children into the football stadium with the large gates that would soon be closed behind them to keep them safe. Inside the stadium, high fences encircled us and floodlights illuminated the compound. There was someone on a highrise stage at one end of the field with a microphone and a record player hooked up to the loud-speaker system that surrounded the stadium. The young leader on stage explained that the children needed to make room for those who had exams the next morning—to allow them to be close to the light to study before lights out and curfew would require them to head to the separated barracks for their few hours of sleep.

Suddenly, a unified sound began to move through the crowd. A beautiful chorus of a thousand voices began to sing. It was hard to make out what they were singing at first, although these hymnal tunes were familiar to me. Uganda is a predominantly Christian country and many of these children obviously had great faith. These thousands of children who had little to sing about were bursting out in song. A powerful emotion swept over me, as I recognized the words of "Blessed Assurance." *This is my story, This is my song, Blessed Assurance all the day long.* This was the same song the all-white congregation had sung at the Edwardsville First Christian church where my dad preached. It was the same song the children had sung at Gethsemane Baptist Church on the other side of the tracks in Edwardsville where Jefferson preached. It was the same song that Jeffie-Lou, Shawne, Sydney, Jefferson, and I all sang at the Little Brown Church in Sequim. How could this be? All these worlds, all these different cultures, all these different children—all of us connected by a hymn, by our faith, and by each other.

These children, the night walkers, validated my journey to date and affirmed my way into the future. During the same time that Joseph Kony was terrorizing the children of Gulu, I continued my own path. Not unlike the night walkers, my own escape became the door to a more promising future. Without my own protectors, I too would have been a victim.

Responding to Natural Disasters, Wars, and Hidden Conflicts

Between 2000 and 2012 natural disasters caused $1.7 trillion in damage and affected 2.9 billion people. The number and severity of natural disasters has quadrupled in the past thirty years. Every year, more than twenty-five million people are directly affected by a natural disaster. Hurricanes, tornadoes, severe flooding, draught, fires, polar vortex, and earthquakes have all become commonplace with no part of the world left untouched by the force of nature.

The effects of conflict and war equally have the world in a vice grip. In Central America, half the population of Guatemala, El Salvador, and Honduras, often referred to as the Central American Forgotten Triangle, live below the poverty line. The region is a powder keg ready to explode.

Colombia has taken a turn for the better with the recent peace accord and deserves the world's support of this very fragile and important negotiated peace agreement. South Sudan, finally an independent state, continues to be plagued by conflict. Burkina Faso, Sierra Leone, and Northern Nigeria are besieged with ongoing violence. Ukraine is in a civil war fueled by Russia, causing significant strain on those forced to live in the affected regions. The terrorist group of Boko Haram, with its stronghold in Northern Nigeria, has terrorized the countryside for almost a decade, killing thousands of innocent people while the government has struggled to fight back. The world's attention only came with the kidnapping of more than 200 school girls in 2014. More recently, Boko Haram attacked a village in the Northeast region of Nigeria, killing at least eighty-six people. When the Nigerian army came to defend the village, they were out armed and failed to stop the killing until additional back-up forces finally arrived.

ISIS, a much larger extremist terrorist movement, took responsibility for a triple bombing, killing dozens of people in a suburb near Syrian's capital. This was merely the latest in a series of atrocities linked to ISIS. The world remains divided on how to stop ISIS, as this terrorist movement continues to wreak havoc not only in Syria but also throughout the Middle East and around the world.

The world is also divided on what to do about Syria and whether to back the Syrian regime of King Assad or the Syrian rebel forces fighting Assad. The flight of the Syrian refugees is of even greater concern, representing what is now considered the largest and not so hidden refugee crisis since World War II.

In September 2014 I was asked to join former President Clinton, King Abdullah II of Jordan, and a distinguished group of NGO and private sector leaders for a commitment at the Clinton Global Initiative to respond to both the immediate and long-term needs of the Syrian refugees. At the time, the Syria refugee crisis was for the most part unknown to the rest of the world, even though the number of refugees has been growing since the outbreak of the Syrian Civil war in 2011.

Global Impact's CGI commitment was to provide a Syrian Refugee fund for raising critical resources and visibility for those responding to the crisis, including Global Impact's Charity Alliance members IRC, IMC, World Vision, and others on the front lines. Raising funds from donors has been difficult. But when the media captured the image of a little boy being washed ashore after drowning in the Mediterranean in his effort to escape to a better life, donors around the world and the United States were finally compelled to respond.

MOAS, The Migrant Offshore Aid Station, a commitment by one entrepreneur to establish a nonprofit and finance a ship that could rescue refugees, is a Global Impact partner. Following the public's attention we have served as the MOAS' fiscal agent for securing more than one million dollars, which has extended MOAS' operations and this life-saving work. MOAS works closely with Doctors Without Borders and others to bring the refugees safely to shore. Unfortunately, the war in Syria has claimed an estimated 400,000 lives, with another 4.5 million

Syrian refugees fleeing the country, and by the end of 2016 the number of Syrians displaced from their homes and communities inside Syria was expected to rise to 8.7 million.

Thankfully, King Hussein Abdullah II and the Hashemite Kingdom of Jordan has continued to fulfill its commitment to take the Syrian refugees—now an estimated 1.4 million of them, disproportionate to the total population and means of this small country. Fortunately, Lebanon and Turkey have also opened their doors to refugees. Due to the leadership of Angela Merkel, Chancellor of Germany and Nobel Peace Prize recipient, an increasing larger number of European countries are accepting larger numbers of Syrian refugees. Hopefully, the United States will also continue to increase the number of refugees who will be accepted. The needs of these refugees for jobs, food, shelter, schooling, and health care are straining the economies of these countries, including Jordan, Lebanon, and Turkey. Women and children are especially being impacted by the crisis.

Funding for the Syrian Refugee crisis has continued to struggle to keep pace with the level of humanitarian response needed. At a recent Global Donors conference, the United States led the way with almost one billion dollars in new aid. The United States is already the largest donor of humanitarian aid to victims of the Syrian conflict, providing an estimated $4.5 billion in food, water, and medical care since the civil war began in 2011. The United Kingdom, Germany, Denmark, Norway, Canada, and Kuwait have also now made significant funding commitments. The private sector is attempting to do its part in providing support for jobs and education for the refugees, including a commitment of $75 million dollars from a diverse range of corporations under the Global Business Coalition for Education.

Meanwhile, the women and children in Gulu, Northern Uganda, and many other parts of the world remain invisible victims of civil unrest and hidden conflict.

GLOBAL GOAL 9

Industry, Innovation and Infrastructure

Build resilient infrastructure, promote inclusive and sustainable industrialization and foster innovation

Ram Bahador Ghalan, a farmer in a remote village near Nepal's Kathmandu valley, had just returned home from tending his crops when he felt the ground tremble under his feet. Within seconds, everything around him was chaos. Bricks, wooden beams, and other debris came raining down. The magnitude 7.8 earthquake was the worst disaster to hit Nepal in eighty years; the quake flattened centuries' old temples and destroyed or damaged over half a million homes. "Everything we own, our clothes, blankets, and food, is buried," Ghalan says, pointing to the pile of bricks that used to be his house.

Charities in Action

ǩamericares

AmeriCares relief workers are among the first to respond and stay as long as needed, helping to restore health services for survivors. Their experience and expertise enables them to conduct multiple responses simultaneously and address remote, challenging situations, which often escape public attention.

The International Rescue Committee (IRC) responds to the world's worst humanitarian crises and helps people survive and rebuild their lives. At work in over 40 countries and 29 U.S. cities to restore safety, dignity and hope, the IRC leads the way from harm to home.

The mission of Doctors Without Borders/Médecins Sans Frontières (MSF) is to provide impartial medical relief to the victims of war, disease, and natural or man-made disaster, without regard to race, religion, or political affiliation.

CHAPTER THIRTEEN

Full Circle

F orty years to the day, I traveled from Washington, DC, to retrace my steps when I ran away from Linwood, Kansas, in the snowstorm in order to return to Sequim, Washington. I was now in my mid-fifties, my hair no longer blonde, now much darker and sprinkled with shades of grey. I had just endured a significant foot injury and surgery, and I made the journey on crutches with a boot still on my injured foot. My first stop was the Claycomo farm, Whitey and Pauline's home, where I had fond memories of eating hamburgers and drinking chocolate shakes and where we had all gathered to decide where to flee to escape the custody suit. The next stop was the barn, and then the store.

The store was now a much more dated thrift store. The McDonald's where Ricky and I used to escape to still stood on the corner across from the store, and that is where I ate a late lunch. I then visited Grandpa and Grandma's grave site at the Liberty Christian Church, where Sydney and Don had started their lives together, where Pauline had written sermons for every minister who served, and where Whitey always made sure to add generously to the offering plate.

Before leaving Claycomo for Liberty, I found my way to see Bill Edward. His home overlooking a lake with ducks and other wildlife was familiar, though the house also showed signs of wear. Bill had been my rescuer those forty years earlier and then continued to be there for me whenever I needed him. I had even borrowed money from Bill for my business. Bill now owned the Claycomo Hughes family farm. He was glad to see me. He was fighting cancer, which would take his life six months later. We both knew it would be the last time we would see each other.

He said, "Scottie, Whitey would be so proud. He always believed you would do great things. Committing your life to others would make him proud—that was what was most important to him."

He confirmed his recollection of the night I ran away and was hidden in his attic. We hugged, took a picture together, and without many words affirmed the greatest gift anyone can give—kindness to another. He had been significant in my life; he made me better. I loved him and he knew it.

The next morning, I set out just before sunrise in the midst of a cold Kansas winter. Snow covered the ground but no blizzard conditions like there had been forty years earlier. After driving across the Missouri River, I made my way to Edwardsville. My first stop was the First Christian Church. Then on to the little parsonage house, which was even smaller than I remembered. A train sped by and I realized that we really had lived close to the tracks. I visited the farm Mom and I once owned and had hoped to remake the rest of our lives. A large mansion had been built on the property. People said the owner had brought the stones from England.

To my surprise, the original tin-roof barn was still standing. The trailer where we lived was long gone, but the tack room—once our living room—was now where the owner kept chickens. I could still imagine the piano with the broken ivory keys that I would play and where I would spend hours practicing hymns and writing my song for my mother.

I visited Gethsemane Church where Jefferson preached, and though it was now abandoned, it felt to me like yesterday, the church full of people, deacons with their white gloves and Jefferson's booming voice. I could imagine the outline of the cross that had smoldered at the entrance of the farm.

I made my way to Bonner Springs and saw the high school where Mom had taught, remembered some of the students, and thought about Michael. Linwood and Tall Oaks was closer to Bonner Springs than I remembered. The little town had fallen on hard times, and the post office where Dad had kept me from getting my letters was now boarded up. The school was still there and the front parking lot where I had once pleaded with my mom *take me with you.*

Tall Oaks campground just outside Linwood was in better condition and looked much the same. The house I remembered was much grander than in reality, but it was still livable. I introduced myself to the current caretaker and knocked on the door at the side of the house, where my Dad had kept his office and his secrets. Whether it was race, religion, the times, my mother's independence and intelligence, or just a bad combination of two young people who never really had a chance of staying together, when I look back as an adult, I have a more comprehensive understanding.

Dad had been raised to want a submissive wife, and Sydney Lou was never going to be that. Part of it was what he had learned from his own father, but another part stemmed from his jealousy of Mom, because they were so different and she was so outgoing and likable. It isn't all about race or about abuse—it's about what each of us does with all that. I have realized that life is short and that the opportunity to forgive is not forever.

I turned to the reason I had come in the first place: to retrace my steps on the night I had run away. Every step from the house to the camp lodge became real again. The pay telephone was no longer there.

Across the meadows, along the tree line, past the swimming pool to the open air chapel, on to the cliffs overlooking the Kansas River. The cliff seemed higher and farther away. I put the crutches back in the rental car, drove around the campground, and picked up the trail by the meadow adjacent to the cliffs. I stood in front of the meadow and pictured where I would have gotten the thorn in my foot. I could see the path down the cliff all the way to the railroad tracks along the river. I crossed the bridge to DeSoto and made my way to the horse ranch.

In all, it was a nine-mile journey. The same distance as the night walker's journey. I didn't know what my life would be like the day I chose to run away and reunite with my mom and Jefferson, but it has been an extraordinary journey.

Reducing the Gap Between Rich and Poor

In 2016, OXFAM, one of Global Impact's Charity Alliance members, reported at DAVOS—home of the World Economic Forum—that 62 people now have as much wealth in total as the poorest 3.6 billion people, or equal to nearly half of the people on the planet.

The economy of the one percent is now the driver of extreme inequality and is ever widening the gap between rich and poor. Regardless of our politics, or where we stand in the continuum, we simply cannot achieve the Global Goals for Sustainability with such inequity. Unless this trend is reversed, we cannot have a better, safer world.

Economic inequity is greater in the United States now than when I was growing up as a child. In the 1960s there was a thriving middle class. Families in the middle income bracket were the majority. Today, those living below the poverty line, rural and urban, constitute the majority.

The poverty I saw in rural Kansas upon my return to Edwardsville to retrace my steps was as poignant and devastating as the poverty I have seen in the West Bank/Gaza Strip, in Northern Uganda, the slums of Nairobi, Kenya, the rural villages of Malawi and Zambia, or the communities living in poverty in Guatemala. The result is that young people living in these conditions will likely never reach their full potential, unless we can close the gap and provide them more opportunities.

GLOBAL GOAL 8

Decent Work and Economic Growth

Promote sustained, inclusive, and sustainable economic growth, full and productive employment, and decent work for all

Most days are the same for women in rural Niger. The work appears never-ending. Santou's life is no different. Her taxing daily routine highlights the challenges of life in the Sahel, a semi-arid region that stretches below the Sahara Desert. Like Santou, most people here depend on subsistence farming, mainly growing the staple grain millet. But increasingly frequent droughts are drying up the land, making every day a struggle to meet the most basic needs. "I want to know there will be enough food for the year. If you have what you need, then you can smile," she says.

Charities in Action

Heifer International contributes to the growth of small and growing businesses (SGBs) in low income countries through the development of pro-poor, wealth-creating value chains in the agriculture sector.

Powered by the belief that a better world is possible, Mercy Corps partners to put bold solution into action—helping people triumph over adversity and build stronger communities from within. Their MicroMentor program guides local entrepreneurs with advice from more experienced counterparts around the world.

ACCION

Accion is a global nonprofit dedicated to building a financially inclusive world with economic opportunity for all, by giving people the financial tools they need to improve their lives. Accion is building the next generation of top-tier microfinance institutions, and over more than 50 years has helped build 65 such institutions in 32 countries on four continents that today reach millions of clients. Its impact investing initiatives are pushing beyond microfinance to catalyze more than 20 innovative start-ups dedicated to improving the efficiency, reach, and scope of financial services for the poor. And its Center for Financial Inclusion is helping to build a stronger industry with high standards and broad engagement. Currently, Accion's work spans nearly two dozen countries, including the U.S., where it is the nation's largest nonprofit microfinance network.

CHAPTER FOURTEEN

A Call to Action

My story is about a boy from a broken home who struggled to become a person with purpose. A boy faced with racism and violence as acceptable ways of life. A boy who finally found his future by having the courage to follow those who loved him, regardless of their social standing or race. It is also the story of millions of children in the United States and around the world whose own journeys from brokenness and inequity required the courage to escape from their conditions and have a better future.

When we look back on our lives, will we have heard and responded to those children who called out "take me with you," loudly or quietly? Were we the significant "other" to a person in need? This book is also my call to action—especially for the millennial generation, whose destiny is not only to be connected but also to change the world for the better. It is my narrative rooted in adversity but also in love and faith. It is about finding the "charity within" and resisting the anger that can overtake everything.

The contributions that you will make are just as important as those that people like Bono and Bill Gates have made. You can—and you will—survive the twists and turns of life. You can contribute in your own way from all walks of life. And for millennials, you are the world's first global generation. You are not bound by race, culture, language, or geography. You are confident, connected to the world, and open to change.

One of the most pressing challenges of our times is global poverty. With more than two billion people living on less than two dollars per day, the disparity between the haves and have-nots throughout the world continues to widen. Unless we seriously address this disparity, it will increasingly impact the global economy, threaten worldwide security, and, perhaps, challenge our very existence.

Interlinked with poverty is the equally pressing issue of human suffering from preventable diseases. Nearly seven million children still die *each year* from preventable causes, including one million who die from diarrhea alone. Three million new people are infected with HIV each year. One million people, mostly young children, die from malaria, despite new technological advances. And one out of every three women in the developing world is undernourished, the effects of which are passed on to their children. Thankfully, we are making progress. Today, with increased awareness and funding, fewer children are dying from unnecessary causes.

We are now at a critical crossroads in which private philanthropy and private sector business solutions will be needed as partners to existing institutional donors and governments if we are to eliminate extreme poverty, achieve gender equality, and meet all of the 17 sustainable development goals, which have now been formally adopted by the United Nations.

There are more success stories to be told. But there is also much more progress to be made, and you must be part of it. The foundation has been laid. The momentum has begun. You are poised to be a game changer and change the world in ways previous generations couldn't imagine. You have the education, ambition, tools, and talent required to meet the global challenge of eliminating poverty and human suffering from unnecessary causes. You can have faith, you can persevere, you can have compassion for others, you can simply do your best, and you will not only succeed—you will make a difference in the world.

I leave you with a call to action. You are the generation of global citizens who will and *must* meet our global challenge. The world is calling you. And you have the opportunity to change the world. Your journey—and your story—is important. Go forth as global citizens. Answer this call to action by sharing your own story with others. Get engaged with the Global Goals for Sustainability and make them personal. Become an advocate for eliminating extreme poverty, rejecting inequality and injustice, and preserving the environment for future generations.

Join the ONE Campaign to Make Poverty History (http://www.one.org/us/). Become a Global Citizen (http://www.theglobalcitizensinitiative.org/). Give to a cause you care about. Be a game changer and establish your own Growfund Giving Account (https://mygrowfund.org/). Contribute to the Global Impact Sustainable Development Goals Fund (charity.org). Take action by committing your time, talent, and treasure to a better, safer world.

Acknowledgments

For those who have been willing to let me share my story with them, you have been my inspiration and I am grateful for you. For those who have committed your own stories to making a difference in the world, you are my inspiration. Putting this story into words has been a decade-long journey. Making it relevant to the world we live in and the world we want has been essential. For the many heroes in my life who, when I would share my story would encourage me to share it with others, I am grateful. To my editing team, Darrick, Joye, and Lara, who helped me shape the story so that others might see themselves in it. I am especially grateful to the talented Lara Asher, who took on the task of the final editing and completion of the manuscript. To Carol Mann and the Carol Mann Agency, and Kenzi Sugihara, President of SelectBooks, who each took a chance on an unknown author.

To Rich Stearns, President of World Vision USA and author; Dr. Chris Elias, President of Global Development for the Bill and Melinda Gates Foundation; and former Congressman Don Bonker, my mentors and friends who wouldn't let me stop until the story was told. To John Oppenheimer, who has been like a brother and was always willing to read the next version of the manuscript. To Scott Burns and Gretchen Sorensen, my good friends, always with a word of encouragement. To my family, who have endured the impact of this story. To my mom and Jeffie Lou, who have never left my side.

To my three daughters and their mom, who are all on their way to change the world in their own journeys.

To my friends and colleagues at Global Impact, who have continued to support me in this endeavor. I am especially grateful to May Samplonius, my executive assistant, who has persevered with me as my partner in the final editing and writing of the narrative. To Joe Mettimano and his team member Brooke Perry, for highlighting the Global Impact Charities and illustrations that symbolize the tremendous work being done around the world. To Ann Canela, who has helped provide input on the arc of the story so it would have meaning to others. To Steve Polo, Global Impact Board Chair, and the Board of Directors for their support. To all of the Global Impact staff and extended family who are game changers in their own rite.

Finally, to all the young men and women of the future generations, who continue to inspire me because they have chosen to find the "charity within" themselves and as a result will change the world for the better. TML.

About the Author

Photo by Elizabeth Dranitzke

SCOTT JACKSON is the President and Chief Executive Officer of Global Impact. Global Impact's mission is to grow global philanthropy and build partnerships and resources for the world's most vulnerable people. It has raised $1.7 billion since inception. A global development fundraising and marketing veteran, Jackson has held leadership positions in the public, private, and non-profit sectors, including the global health and development non-profits PATH and World Vision. He has worked in more than sixty-five countries, and his global relief and development efforts have taken him to remote villages in Africa and Asia, to the heart of the Holy Land, and inside some of the most powerful institutions and governments around the world. Jackson has worked with global leaders around the world, including four US presidents and their administrations, and he has represented international development issues with the offices of US Secretaries of State Madeleine Albright, Colin Powell, and Hillary Clinton.

Jackson was a founding member of the nonprofit organization ONE Campaign to "make poverty history" and has worked on initiatives with Bono and the Bill and Melinda Gates Foundation. He is a long-standing member of the Clinton Global Initiative, and he serves on several national boards, including the International Center for Research on Women and the U.S. Fund for UNICEF. He currently works closely with the leadership of more than one hundred twenty nonprofits around the world, such as Save the Children, CARE, and Doctors Without Borders. He has traveled to Uganda to raise awareness about war criminal Joseph Kony. Beyond Africa, Jackson has assisted with major relief efforts in the West Bank and Gaza Strip, in New York City after 9/11, in New Orleans post-Katrina, and in Manhattan after Hurricane Sandy. He's worked to fight famine in North Korea and preventable disease throughout the developing world.

Jackson has worked on global poverty and global development issues with many individuals and organizations, including Nelson Mandela, Desmond Tutu, Al Gore, Saddleback Church's Rick Warren and Focus on the Family's James Dobson, and civil rights leaders Jesse Jackson and Al Sharpton. He's a trusted and influential behind-the-scenes voice, whose opinions and insights have spanned political, religious, and racial divisions and helped shape policies at the highest levels for more than three decades.

Before taking leadership roles in the global development humanitarian sector, Scott founded TRADEC (Trade and Development Consortium), one of the first marketing and communications firms in North America to specialize in international trade and development, which later became part of APCO, a worldwide communications firm. During his early career, Jackson served as assistant to a US congressman, and he held a number of roles in national politics. He has appeared in *The New York Times, The Washington Post*, and *The Huffington Post.*

In October 2016 Jackson was awarded the Gelman, Rosenberg and Freedman CEO EXCEL Award by the Center for Nonprofit Advancement. The award recognizes leadership achievement in the areas of innovation, motivation, community building, ethical integrity, and strategic leadership.

Jackson received an MBA from the University of Edinburgh School of International Business. He also holds an honorary Doctorate of Humane Letters from the University of Puget Sound, where he received a Bachelor of Arts in history. He lives in Washington, DC.